sharing with travellers a wealth of
experience and a passion for travel.

**Rely on Thomas Cook as your
travelling companion on your next trip
and benefit from our unique heritage.**

Thomas Cook **pocket** guides

COPENHAGEN

Your travelling companion since 1873

Thomas
Cook

Written by Pat Levy
Updated by Nicol Foulkes

Published by Thomas Cook Publishing
A division of Thomas Cook Tour Operations Limited
Company registration No: 3772199 England
The Thomas Cook Business Park, 9 Coningsby Road
Peterborough PE3 8SB, United Kingdom
Email: books@thomascook.com, Tel: +44 (0)1733 416477
www.thomascookpublishing.com

Produced by The Content Works Ltd
Aston Court, Kingsmead Business Park, Frederick Place
High Wycombe, Bucks HP11 1LA
www.thecontentworks.com

Series design based on an original concept by Studio 183 Limited

ISBN: 978-1-84848-285-2

First edition © 2006 Thomas Cook Publishing
This third edition © 2010 Thomas Cook Publishing
Text © Thomas Cook Publishing
Maps © Thomas Cook Publishing/PCGraphics (UK) Limited
Transport map © Communicarta Limited

Series Editor: Lucy Armstrong
Production/DTP: Steven Collins

Printed and bound in Spain by GraphyCems

Cover photography (Tivoli Gardens) © Paul Panayiotou/Alamy

CONTENTS

SYMBOLS KEY

The following symbols are used throughout this book:

ⓐ address ⓣ telephone ⓦ website address ⓛ opening times
ⓝ public transport connections ⓘ important

The following symbols are used on the maps:

ⓘ information office		▣ points of interest
✈ airport		O city
✚ hospital		O large town
⛊ police station		○ small town
▣ bus station		═ motorway
▤ railway station		▬ main road
Ⓜ metro		▬ minor road
✝ cathedral		— railway
❶ numbers denote featured cafés & restaurants			

Hotels and restaurants are graded by approximate price as follows:
£ budget price ££ mid-range price £££ expensive £££+ most expensive

▶ *The Copenhagen Botanical Gardens' glasshouse and pond*

INTRODUCING
Copenhagen

Introduction

Dynamic yet quaint. Small and compact, yet complex and rich.
Pedestrianised streets, wide, ancient city squares and festivals
galore. Copenhagen, Denmark's capital and arguably Scandinavia's
liveliest city, will keep you entertained all year round.

You'll immediately notice how laid-back the people of Copenhagen
are. The locals love to enjoy life, so there are countless cafés and bars,
numerous well-kept parks, and vibrant harbour and beach areas.
It is a happy city, comfortable with itself and its place in the world.

It is a clean, healthy city to visit, too. A car is the last thing you
will want, as you can walk from one area to another in half an hour.
You can hire a bike and spin around with the rest of the eco-friendly
inhabitants. If that is too energetic, you can hop on the speedy and
efficient designer metro. Copenhagen is well on its way to becoming
the first capital city in the world to be CO_2 neutral, with almost
40 per cent of its residents cycling to work, energy-efficient street
lighting and wind farms in the sea and surrounding countryside.

Culture and design are two of Copenhagen's finest qualities.
You'll see cutting-edge displays of architectural, interior and fashion
design, both ancient and modern, thanks in part to Denmark's Royal
Family, the Carlsberg Foundation and the city's other illustrious
benefactors.

Food culture has evolved rapidly over the past few years with plenty
of organic options, a range of Danish and international cuisine, and
12 Michelin-starred restaurants.

Music is everywhere in this fun-loving city, and there are regular
live performances from local talents and big names. Don't miss the
popular annual Jazz Festival (see page 12).

And there is mindless pleasure too. If that is your thing, come to the Tivoli Gardens, a little 21st-century Eden where all is well in the world. You'll find computer games alongside giant puppets, stomach-churning rides beside kitsch merry-go-rounds. Here, Hans Christian Andersen's well-loved fairy stories have no darker side.

But whatever you do in Copenhagen, you'll have to try hard for your visit, like a fairy story, not to end happily ever after.

🔺 *Hans Christian Andersen statue on Rådhuspladsen*

When to go

Summer days in Copenhagen are long and bright, and winter evenings can be long and dark. Summer is the time when Copenhageners leave the city and foreign visitors flock to it, for the host of festivals, entertainment and events around the harbour and canals. Some sights may close during winter. Come for the Christmas market, though, when the city is lit up and has a warm, magical spirit, in spite of the cooler temperatures.

SEASONS & CLIMATE

Winters are a few degrees colder than in Britain, but still relatively mild. Snow rarely arrives now before February or March. Be warned that the temperature in winter is unpredictable, and frequently fluctuates more than 10°C (50°F) in one day.

Spring is chilly but bright, and the driest time of year. The temperature in summer peaks at around 30°C (86°F), but it rains more, and can be humid. Towards September expect mild sunny days.

Autumn barely happens, and by November the temperature is back to single figures.

ANNUAL EVENTS

January

New Year Celebrations in Rådhuspladsen and firework displays all over town. Lots of concerts leading up to midnight.

February–March

Copenhagen Fashion Week Fashion shows and events both indoors and out, with one weekend of free events for the public. Also held in August. ⓦ www.copenhagenfashionweek.com

Dyrehavsbakken (Bakken Amusement Park) officially opens for the season on the last Thursday in March. Hundreds of motorcyclists congregate in Nørrebro and head out to Bakken in convoy.
🅐 Dyrehavsbakken, Klampenborg ☎ 39633544 🆆 www.bakken.dk

April–May
CPH:PIX Ten-day international feature film festival, with workshops and seminars as well as films. 🆆 www.cphpix.com
Queen Margrethe II's birthday The Queen appears on the balcony at Amalienborg Slot at noon on 16 Apr and the Royal Guard parades in ceremonial uniform.
Tivoli Gardens opens for the summer season. 🆆 www.tivoli.dk

🔺 *Amalienborg Palace*

May Day Parade to Fælled Park by trade unionists and workers. Speeches, music events, food stalls and lots of ale.

Copenhagen Architecture and Design Days (Cph ADD) Events and exhibitions throughout the city over three days in early May. Ⓦ www.cphadd.com

Ølfestival (Beer festival) over three days at Valby Hallen. Ⓦ www.ale.dk

Copenhagen Marathon Over 26 years old, the Copenhagen marathon circles the city on a Sunday in mid-May. Ⓦ www.copenhagenmarathon.com

Whitsun Carnival Parade from Strøget to Fælledparken. Three days of Latin American fun and world music. Ⓦ www.karneval.dk

June–July

Trixxx – Christiania Festival Two days of music, dancing, film, art, political debate and experimental design and architecture. Ⓦ www.trixxx.dk

Sankt Hans Aften The longest day of the year is 23 June. Bonfires and parties on the beaches and in the parks.

Roskilde Festival Rock festival with 70,000 or more visitors, big names, stalls, camping, mud and chemical toilets. Late June–July. ❸ Dyrskuepladsen, Darupvej ❶ 46366613 Ⓦ www.roskilde-festival.dk

Jazz Festival Ten days of indoor and outdoor performances around the city (see page 12).

August–October

Copenhagen Pride Week Gay pride parade and a week of events in mid-Aug. Ⓦ www.copenhagenpride.dk

Cultural Night Museums, theatres and galleries are open late and free of charge on the first night of the school autumn term. Ⓦ www.kulturnatten.dk

Copenhagen Cooking (Nordic Food Festival) Scandinavia's largest food festival. Special menu at selected restaurants. Late Aug–early Sept. Ⓦ www.copenhagencooking.dk

November–December
CPH:DOX International documentary film festival. Ⓦ www.cphdox.dk
Copenhagen Autumn Jazz in clubs throughout the city, early Nov.
ⓘ 33932013 Ⓦ www.jazzfestival.dk
Christmas Parade to light the tree in Rådhuspladsen, last Sat in Nov.
Ⓦ www.visitcopenhagen.com
Tivoli Christmas Market Christmas shopping, ice skating, good eating and a glass of *gløgg* (mulled wine). Mid-Nov–Christmas. Ⓦ www.tivoli.dk

PUBLIC HOLIDAYS
Nytårs dag (New Year's Day) 1 Jan
Skærtorsdag, Langfredag, 2 Påskedag (Maundy Thursday, Good Friday & Easter Monday) 1, 2, 5 Apr 2010, 21, 22, 25 Apr 2011, 5, 6, 9 Apr 2012
Stor Bededag (Common Prayer Day) 4th Fri after Good Friday
Kristi himmelfartsdag (Ascension Day) 13 May 2010, 2 June 2011, 17 May 2012
2 Pinsedag (Whit Monday) 24 May 2010, 13 June 2011, 28 May 2012
Juleferie (Christmas) 24–26 Dec

Public transport runs to Sunday schedules, and banks, post offices and public buildings are closed on these days. Grundlovsdag (Constitution Day) on 5 June is not an official public holiday, but some shops and businesses do close.

The Jazz Festival

Copenhagen's most celebrated event is the annual Jazz Festival, a local institution since 1978. It takes place over ten days in July, starting on the first Friday. Whether you're a jazz enthusiast, or someone who likes to hear it in the background at a trendy bar, don't miss this event.

During the festival, every possible space in the city becomes a venue. The big names play at the Opera House (see page 99), the Gamle Scene (see page 64), the Playhouse (see page 70) and Koncerthuset (see page 28), but cafés, parks, public squares, churches, and even museums are a stage for the hundreds of performers who flock here. You will hear all kinds of jazz, from traditional to experimental.

The big concerts can be expensive, but they're worth it. Cafés and clubs only charge a small entrance fee, and open-air events are free. Some of the best small performances are those by Denmark's home-grown jazz musicians.

The rich history of jazz in Copenhagen adds a telling dimension. During World War II, the music became a form of resistance to the German occupation. In the 1960s, the great American jazz musicians heard about Denmark's reputation for liberality and permissiveness and found their way here. Some of them made it their home, and perhaps this explains the quality and intensity of local talent as well as the enthusiasm of those who listen to it.

Household names – Dizzie Gillespie, Ray Charles, Ella Fitzgerald, Oscar Peterson, Winton Marsalis – have played here. Future household names are still coming. The festival hosts top American, Brazilian, Argentinean, Austrian and Scandinavian artists, and proudly showcases an extensive line-up of local talent.

Copenhagen is a wonderful place to be in summer anyway. But the Jazz Festival takes life out onto the streets, and a sunny, laughing,

THE JAZZ FESTIVAL

relaxed chaos hits the city. The music and atmosphere have become so popular that the city now holds another festival, Autumn Jazz, in early November.

The city's accommodation gets packed during the festival, so make sure you book early.

Copenhagen Jazz Festival ⓐ Sankt Peder Stræde 28C ⓣ 33932013 ⓦ www.jazz.dk

🔺 *July sees jazz all over the city – afloat, on the streets, wherever there's space*

History

Like all fairytale heroes, Copenhagen had humble beginnings. In the 12th century it was just a scruffy hamlet called Havn, surrounded on all sides by salt marshes and reliant upon fishing for trade. The dominant city in Denmark was Roskilde (see page 126), with its stone cathedral and kings.

It was piracy that gave Copenhagen its break. In 1167 King Valdemar I sent his brother Bishop Absalon to sort out pirates who were attacking shipping in the area. Havn's strategic position was perfect for controlling the Øresund, Denmark's narrow shipping channel, and Bishop Absalon quickly built a fortress there. Thus Copenhagen was founded.

The city's growth has been turbulent. A couple of centuries after its foundation, Copenhagen's *Köbmandshavn* (merchant's harbour), was being attacked regularly by its neighbours for its strategic importance. In 1443 the Danish kings moved their capital there. In 1536, during the peasants' revolt, Copenhagen was besieged. The city's residents ate rats for a while, then gave this up and surrendered quickly to the king's forces. In the same year, Denmark broke away from the Roman Catholic church.

It was only in the 16th century that Christian IV began the first proper building projects, such as Christianshavn (see page 90), the Rundetårn, the Børsen, old stock exchange (see page 90), and Rosenborg Slot (Rosenborg Castle) (see page 108). A lot of the city was subsequently destroyed by a fire in 1728 and a 30-year war with its neighbours. A plague wiped out 20,000 inhabitants of the city around the same time. Copenhagen didn't have it easy.

It didn't get much better in the 19th century when there was another seige, this time by Admiral Lord Nelson. A fledgling cultural renaissance, centred around the writer Hans Christian Andersen, the philosopher Søren Kierkegaard and the sculptor Thorvaldsen, was overcome by the industrial revolution which hit Copenhagen at the same time. Workers flocked to the city, poverty and squalor increased, and Vesterbro and Nørrebro were created as workers' homes.

In 1940 Germany invaded. Five years of occupation followed, but Denmark, uniquely in Europe, managed to rescue the vast majority of its Jews.

The war marked a turning point in Copenhagen's economic and social history. A nationwide social welfare programme was instituted, and in the 1960s Denmark boomed. Immigrant workers rushed to take up new employment opportunities. The first skyscraper, the Radisson Hotel, went up. Copenhagen's youth joined protests about the nuclear bomb, Vietnam and education. Pornography was legalised.

The 1970s saw the establishment of the free state of Christiania (see page 92) in a disused army base, and Denmark joined the European Economic Community. In 2000 the building of the Øresund Bridge linked Copenhagen with Sweden by road and rail, reinforcing its position as an economic and social power. A conservative government and some religious tensions have recently challenged Denmark's celebrated tradition of openness and acceptance. But if history teaches us anything, it is that Copenhagen's future will be anything but dull and predictable.

○ *Early Danish headgear, National Museum*

Lifestyle

Copenhagen's history helps us to understand the lifestyle and attitudes of its people today. It hasn't been a cheerful and easy one, with its pirates, fires, plagues, sieges, occupations and unrest. Now Copenhageners want a bit of law and order. For a simple yet telling example, look out for their quasi-religious obedience of pedestrian crossing signals.

The anarchy which used to exist in the heart of the city is slowly being phased out, and Copenhagen is moving into the 21st century. Christiania displays this transformation in action. On the one hand, Christiania is a genuinely anarchist society, run along democratic lines. Crime is kept low not by the law but by cooperation between the residents. The community pays little or nothing in rent and taxes, and looks after itself happily. Young people spend their weekends enjoying the atmosphere. On the other hand, Christiania is prime real estate, and several successful businesses are already established

SOCIAL ETIQUETTE

Copenhagen's social rules spring from a paradoxical mixture of respect for law and order, and democratic anarchy. Here are a couple of tips.

Obey pedestrian crossing signals and keep out of cycle lanes. Observe every British rule about queuing, except, oddly, at bus stops. It's best not to offend residents by taking photographs in Christiania, as if it's a tourist attraction. And remember that everyone is equal in Copenhagen. Don't expect waiters or cleaners to grovel.

there. The fascinating social experiment it represents won't last all that long. So visit now (see page 92).

Law, order, anarchy and, more importantly, *hygge*. This is a specifically Danish concept, meaning 'cosiness' or 'togetherness'. It conjures up the idea of keeping the forces of darkness at bay with good cheer, of social responsibility and looking after one another. On a political level, Denmark's great social welfare system sums this up. On a social level, see it everywhere at Tivoli (see page 80) and during the Jazz Festival (see page 12).

◔ *A couple having a heart-to-heart at the Three Lakes*

Culture

Copenhagen arguably leads the world in interior design. Perhaps that is not surprising. *Hygge*, or 'cosiness' (see Lifestyle section), also means the need to create a secure and happy environment.

As you'll see, Danish furniture, cutlery and other home furnishings manage to combine form with function. The well-known Danish egg chair, for example, provides ultimate comfort with a simple, flowing grace. Arne Jacobsen's smooth steel teapots are beautiful to look at, and don't dribble tea. The silversmith Georg Jensen has produced beautiful silver pieces of jewellery and silverware along similar flowing lines. Nowadays Danish design is still thriving, particularly in Copenhagen, with shops all over selling fine glassware and lamps, furniture and other home furnishings.

The country has other cultural highs too, in music, literature, theatre, arts and cinema. Copenhagen, as its vibrant capital, has the best of them all. The 21st century brought about change for the Danish Royal Theatre (see page 64). Previously most stage performances of opera, theatre, ballet and orchestra were held at what is now called the Gamle Scene (Old Stage, see page 64) in Kongens Nytorv, but in 2005 a new Opera House was built (see page 99), followed in 2008 by the chic harbourside Skuespilhuset (Playhouse, see page 70). Construction of the Playhouse began in 2004 after the Ministry for Cultural Affairs launched an international design competition for the new theatre which was won by Danish architects Boje Lundgaard and Lene Tranberg. The stunning building, both inside and out, was completed in a little over three years at a cost of 900 million Danish kroner.

As well as hosting two of the best rock and jazz festivals in Europe, the city has a lively traditional classical music scene. Resident

⬢ Humble items but great design at the Dansk Design Center

⬤ *Cutting-edge design for the stunning modern Opera House*

orchestras include the Zealand Symphony Orchestra and the Danish National Symphony Orchestra. In mid-August the city presents a free open-air operatic performance, sometimes combined with ballet or theatre, in one of the bigger parks in the city. Previous performances have been held at Fælledparken, Søndermarken and Rosenborg Ekserceplads (next to Kongens Have).

Theatre is both conservative and avante-garde. Det Kongelige Teater (the Royal Theatre, see page 64) is a popular theatre and also the home of the Danish Royal Ballet Company. The London Toast Theatre (see page 30) puts on light comedies in English.

Denmark has long been recognized for its film culture, so it should come as no surprise that there are numerous cinemas and various film festivals throughout the year. Films are always shown in their original language with subtitles.

▶ *Strøget is Denmark's, and Europe's, longest pedestrianised shopping street*

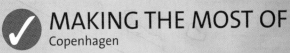

MAKING THE MOST OF
Copenhagen

Shopping

Thankfully, Copenhagen isn't filled with cheap, tacky souvenirs. But it is the place to spend time and money finding something valuable.

Danish design is everywhere, in everyday items such as cutlery, pots and pans, table lamps and clothes. Try shops such as Illums Bolighus, Georg Jensen and Royal Copenhagen on the main shopping street Strøget. Go for some Arne Jacobsen-designed steel items such as his ashtray, coffee pot or vacuum flask. **Royal Copenhagen** porcelain (Ⓦ www.royalcopenhagen.com) is very collectible. Georg Jensen shops sell inventive and original jewellery. For clothes, you'll find the city is full of boutiques and vintage clothes shops with designs and sizes to suit all tastes.

Choose the perfect gift for children from hundreds of cut paper mobiles, many featuring events from Hans Christian Andersen stories. And if you go at the right time of year, Copenhagen sells the best Christmas decorations in Europe.

Strøget and the surrounding streets are the best places to start

SHOPPING HOURS

Shops generally open on weekdays around 10.00–10.30 and close between 17.00 and 19.00, sometimes 20.00 on Friday. On Saturdays, most places except large department stores close at 14.00 or 15.00, except on the first Saturday of the month, when they stay open until 17.00 or 18.00. During summer, many shops in the city centre open on Sunday, but during the rest of the year they only open on the first Sunday of the month until 17.00 or 18.00.

USEFUL SHOPPING PHRASES

What time does the shop open/close?
Hvornår åbner/lukker butikken?
Vohnor orbna/lorka boo-teeken?

How much is this?
Hvor meget koster det?
Vohr mah-eht kosta di?

I'll take this
Jeg tager den her
Yai ta denn hair

This is too large/too small. Do you have any others?
Den er for stor/lille. Har du andre?
Dehn air fo store/lilla. Hah do andera?

shopping, while the pedestrianised streets of Nørrebro have lots of funky clothes, antiques and design shops. Istegade is the place for fetish gear and trendy shoe and clothes shops. Bredgade is known for upmarket design and antiques.

Christiania is worth browsing for young, trendy presents, while Islands Brygge is great for kooky clothes by local designers. Take a wander down Gammel Kongevej for more designer clothing, organic food stores and classic Scandinavian interior design shops. Copenhagen also has several excellent weekend flea markets.

Eating & drinking

Whether you just want a quick snack or a light lunch, whether you prefer to spend the evening over a beer and a good dinner, or whether you fancy treating yourself to a luxurious six-course haute cuisine piece of culinary art, there is something for you in Copenhagen. Twelve restaurants boasting Michelin stars is a lot for a small city, and there are many more great establishments at the cutting edge of Danish fusion cooking.

Traditional Danish cuisine is mostly based on meat, in particular pork, beef and duck. Venison often appears on the menu too. Fish is popular, especially pollock, hake, mackerel and herring, and dishes are

usually served with potatoes and root vegetables. Danes enjoy dense, dark bread and a wide variety of cheeses. *Smørrebrød* is an open sandwich traditionally made with rye or wheat bread and piled high with cold meats or herring, garnished with pickled vegetables or salad.

Eating out in Copenhagen's luxury restaurants is not cheap, but it's a real treat. Often, they serve a fusion of French and Danish kitchen, blending traditional Danish ingredients with French specialities such as foie gras. Some unusual foods appear on your plate in the very upmarket restaurants – chickweed or nasturtium flowers, for example.

● *Enjoy the harbour view and Opera House from your table at Custom House*

PRICE CATEGORIES

Based on the average price per head for a three-course dinner,
excluding drinks. Lunch will usually be a little cheaper in
each category.

£ up to 300kr   ££ 300–500kr   £££ over 500kr

Fortunately for your wallet, cheap, good, fun places serving
hearty, well-cooked food abound. Café bars offer loaded sandwiches,
burgers and often a daily pasta or wok dish. Ethnic restaurants have
taken off, especially in Nørrebro and Vesterbro. Thai restaurants and
sushi bars are popular.

European cafés are everywhere, and many have their own
specialities in food, cocktails, wine, coffee, music, interior design,
or art. Most of them are open until around midnight, but stop
serving food between 21.00 and 22.00. In *smørrebrød* bars you
can enjoy a traditional open sandwich.

If you want to have a meal in one of the parks, or by the harbour
or beachside, you can get great meals to go from many cafés,
authentic Italian pizzerias and the top-class delis which are popping
up in Vesterbro, Nørrebro, Frederiksberg and Christianshavn. Or you
can make your own. All over the city there are good delicatessens
and supermarkets where you can buy bread, cheese, cold meats and
pickles, and bakeries selling hot bread, *wienerbrød* (Danish pastries),
filled sandwiches and coffee.

The Danes have a strong beer culture, and locally brewed beers
are popular. Wine lists in restaurants are impressive, but often
expensive. One traditional drink to try when eating a *smørrebrød*
is *akvavit*, an astringent liqueur which is thrown down as quickly as

USEFUL DINING PHRASES

I would like a table for ... people, please
Et bord til ..., tak
It boorr ti ..., tack

I am a vegetarian
Jeg er vegetar
Yai air veggehtar

Where is the toilet (restroom) please?
Hvor er toilettet, tak?
Vohr air toylehdeht, tack?

Can I pay, please?
Må jeg betale, tak?
Moy ya' betailah, tack?

Do you accept credit cards?
Tager I kreditkort?
Tah ee krehdeetkort?

possible and followed by a beer chaser. For an after-dinner digestif, try *Gammel Dansk* (Old Danish).

There is no need to leave elaborate tips. It is usual to round up the bill to the nearest 10kr or leave 10 or 20kr for the waiter. Your credit card receipt will usually have a space for you to write in a tip if you wish.

Entertainment & nightlife

With a young, fun-loving population and a constant flow of visitors, the city's nightlife scene leaves nothing to be desired. Like its range of restaurants, Copenhagen's club scene has grown to match its increasing wealth and its ethnic and libertarian influences. Most musical tastes are catered to and clubs and discos exist to suit every lifestyle, wallet and age group.

Some of Copenhagen's café bars metamorphose at night into clubs, and some clubs open during the day. Most clubs go in and out of fashion, but places such as **Vega** (ⓐ Enghavevej 40 ❶ 33257011 ⓦ www.vega.dk) are still going strong after many years. Vega, indeed, receives government subsidies.

Clubs get going quite late, especially at weekends when they are empty until well past 01.00. This may be because drinking all night and into the early hours would be prohibitively expensive. Many clubs have a lower age limit of 21. Check out ⓦ www.aok.dk for details of what's on.

If you prefer violins and flutes to ear-splitting hip-hop and house, you'll be pleased to know that Copenhagen offers many opportunities to enjoy classical concerts. Major venues for classical musical performances include:

Christianskirke ⓐ Strandgade 1 ❶ 32541576 ⓦ www.christianskirke.dk

Holmens Kirke (Navy Church) gives regular concerts and special performances at Easter and Christmas (see page 96).

Koncerthuset The home of the Danish National Symphony Orchestra gives live performances every Thursday during the concert season, which stretches from August to May. ⓐ DR Byen, Emil Holms Kanal ❶ 35206262 ⓦ www.dr.dk/koncerthuset

Det Kongelige Teater (see page 64)

Den Sorte Diamant (The Black Diamond) (see page 98)

Tivolis Koncertsal (see page 80)

Copenhagen has a lively modern dance scene, with several small companies offering innovative programmes of contemporary dance. Venues for modern dance include:

Dansescenen ⓐ Østerfælled Torv 34 ❶ 35438300/35432021 ⓦ www.dansescenen.dk

Kanonhallen ⓐ Kigurren 1–3 ❶ 35432324 ⓦ www.kanonhallen.net

Tivoli (see page 80)

You may find that a spell of cold or rainy weather during your trip makes you just want to relax in front of a good film in a cosy cinema. If so, you're in luck. Copenhagen has cinema from multiplex to art house. Films are shown in the original language and subtitled in Danish, and you can take alcohol in with you.

Cinemaxx ⓐ Fisketorvet Shopping Centre, Kalvebod Brygge ❶ 70101202 ⓦ www.cinemaxx.dk

Empire Bio ⓐ Guldbergsgade 29f ❶ 35360036 ⓦ www.empirebio.dk

Gloria ⓐ Rådhuspladsen 59 ❶ 33124292 ⓦ www.gloria.dk

Grand Teatret ⓐ Mikkel Bryggers Gade 8 ❶ 33151611 ⓦ www.grandteatret.dk

Palads ⓐ Axeltorv 9 ❶ 70131211 ⓦ www.biobooking.dk

Park Bio ⓐ Østerbrogade 79 ❶ 35383362 ⓦ www.parkbio-kbh.dk

Theatre is also popular. There are numerous stages scattered throughout Copenhagen, the most impressive being:

Det Kongelige Teater (see page 64)

Det Ny Teater (The New Theatre) ⓐ Gammel Kongevej 29 ❶ 33255075 ⓦ www.detnyteater.dk

Operaen (Opera House) (see page 99)

Skuespilhuset (Playhouse) (see page 70)

● *Det Kongelige Teater at Kongens Nytorv*

Even if you don't speak any Danish and don't fancy spending an evening wondering desperately what the actors are saying, don't write off the city's performing arts scene. For plays in English, try:

London Toast Theatre ⊚ Kochsvej 18 ❶ 33228686
Ⓦ www.londontoast.dk

That Theatre Company ⊚ Axeltorv 12 ❶ 33135042 Ⓦ www.that-theatre.com

NO SMOKING

In 2007 Denmark joined many other countries in Europe in banning smoking in public places, including restaurants and bars. However, in some cases the Danes are prepared to bend (or break) the rules, so you may find the occasional bar where the proprietor still allows smoking indoors.

It's easy to find out what's on in Copenhagen during your stay, and to buy tickets for forthcoming performances. The English-language weekly newspaper *Copenhagen Post* has information about performances and events in the city. Find free copies in cafés and shops or check Ⓦ www.cphpost.dk. *Copenhagen This Week* is a free monthly publication containing events listings, available online at Ⓦ www.ctw.dk.

Billetlugen sells tickets online and at any of the FONA (electrical) stores. Ⓦ www.billetlugen.dk

Billetnet sells tickets online, by telephone, and at any post office. ❶ 38481122 Ⓦ www.billetnet.dk

E-Billet, for e-tickets to some concerts and cinemas. Ⓦ www.e-billet.dk

Tivoli Billetcenter at the entrance to Tivoli Gardens sells tickets for Tivoli and other events. ❸ Vesterbrogade 3 ❶ 33151012 ❹ 09.00–20.00 during Tivoli opening hours (see page 82)

If you want to enjoy yourself in Copenhagen without overspending, consider getting a CPHCARD. Available from any tourist office for periods of 24 or 72 hours, the card offers unlimited public transport around the city (so you can easily hop from bar to bar) and discounts at many cultural institutions and places of entertainment. See Ⓦ www.visitcopenhagen.com.

Sport & relaxation

SPECTATOR SPORTS

Football

Match seasons run from late July to November and from March to early June. There are two main teams playing at different stadiums. **Brøndby IF** (ⓐ Brøndby Stadion 30, Brøndby ⓣ 43630810 ⓦ www.brondby.com) tickets cost 110–220kr. **FC København** (ⓐ Parken, Øster Allé 50 ⓣ 35437400 ⓦ www.fck.dk) play at the national stadium. Tickets cost from 80kr for national games up to 400kr for international games and are available from Billetlugen (see page 31).

Handball

Dansk Håndbold Forbund (Danish Handball Association ⓣ 43262400 ⓦ www.dhf.dk) are based at the Brøndby Stadion (see above).

Ice hockey

Rungsted Cobras (ⓐ Stadionallé 11, Rungsted Kyst ⓣ 45763031 ⓦ www.rik.dk) season runs from November to March.

PARTICIPATION SPORTS

Ice skating

Winter is the time for ice skating in Copenhagen, with outdoor rinks set up around the city in Kongens Nytorv, Tivoli, Blågårdsplads and several other locations. There is an indoor skating rink at **Østerbro Skøjtehal** (ⓐ Per Henrik Lings Allé 6 ⓣ 35421865 ⓛ 12.00–14.45 Mon–Fri, 16.00–18.30 Sun).

Jogging

Joggers use most of the parks in the city as well as the Three

Lakes and the harbour area between Langebro Bridge and Fisketorv shopping centre. It is safe to jog alone at sensible times and when other people are around.

Sports & fitness centres

DGI-Byen Family-friendly, modern sports centre with courts for ball games, an enormous pool, a bowling alley and spa facilities. ⓐ Tietensgade 63 ❶ 33298000 Ⓦ www.dgi-byen.dk ❶ 06.30–23.00 Mon–Thur, 06.30–20.00 Fri, 09.00–20.00 Sat, 09.00–18.00 Sun (opening hours vary)

Fitness dk Denmark's largest fitness centre chain found at numerous locations in Copenhagen. ❶ 39129900 Ⓦ www.fitnessdk.dk

SATS A chain of fitness centres located throughout the city. ❶ 36933000 Ⓦ www.sats.com

Swimming

For indoor swimming try DGI-Byen (see above) and **Frederiksberg Svømmehal** (ⓐ Helgesvej 29 ❶ 38140400 Ⓦ www.frederiksberg svoemmehal.dk) with spa facilities and child-friendly pools.

For outdoor swimming, try one of the city's two harbour bathing areas. **Copacabana – Havnebad ved Fisketorvet** (ⓐ Havneholmen Ⓦ www.islands-bryggge.com ❶ 11.00–19.00 June–Aug) is made up of several floating bridges and contains three bathing areas: one for kids, one for serious swimmers, and one diving pool. **Københavns Havnebad Islands Brygge** (ⓐ Islands Brygge Ⓦ www.islands-bryggge.com ❶ 07.00–19.00 Mon–Fri, 11.00–19.00 Sat & Sun, June–Aug) has five swimming areas: two for kids, two 50 m (164 ft) pools, and one diving pool. If you don't feel like swimming then just relax in the sun with the other visitors to Islands Brygge.

Accommodation

The main accommodation areas are around Central Station, Nyhavn and Nørreport. The number of hotel rooms in Copenhagen has more than doubled since 1999 and the city's accommodation is becoming known for its state-of-the-art-design. Accommodation for all budgets can be found in hotels, self-catering apartments, youth hostels and B&Bs within the city, and in campsites, manor houses and guesthouses outside the city. The usual 1- to 5-star rating system applies.

Turning up in Copenhagen without a reservation can be risky, as during the summer and well into September rooms are usually fully booked. Also, be aware of any events happening in the city as prices rocket and accommodation is often booked up. The best deals are to be found via the internet or through the booking agency in the tourist information centre, Copenhagen Right Now (see page 150).

Prices for rooms in B&Bs are between 280 and 550kr per night and can be found through **Dansk Bed & Breakfast** (ⓐ Sankt Peders Stræde 41 ❶ 39610405 ⓦ www.bbdk.dk). As a cheaper alternative to B&B accommodation, consider staying in one of Copenhagen's many excellent value hostels or 'sleep-inns' (see page 38).

PRICE CATEGORIES

Based on the average cost of a double room in the high season.

£ up to 600kr ££ 600–1,000kr £££ 1,000–1400kr
£££+ over 1,400kr

HOTELS

Cab Inn City £ Central and clean, but with tiny rooms. Lounge area, 24-hour reception, helpful staff. See also its sister hotels Cab Inn Scandinavia or Cab Inn Copenhagen, both in Frederiksberg. ⓐ Mitchellsgade 14 (Rådhuspladsen & the West) ❶ 33461616 ⓦ www.cabinn.com

Hotel Selandia £–£££+ Central and popular, with comfortable rooms and free wireless internet. ⓐ Helgolandsgade 12 (Rådhuspladsen & the West) ❶ 33314610 ⓦ www.hotel-selandia.dk

Hotel Jørgensen ££ Simply furnished, spotless rooms. Dormitory accommodation also available. ⓐ Rømersgade 11 (Around the Three Lakes) ❶ 33138186 ⓦ www.hoteljoergensen.dk

Hotel Nora ££ Old apartment block on the Nørrebro side of the lakes. ⓐ Nørrebrogade 18C (Around the Three Lakes) ❶ 35372021 ⓦ www.hotelnora.dk

Sømandshjemmet Bethel ££ Former seaman's hostel. ⓐ Nyhavn 22 (Nyhavn area) ❶ 33130370 ⓦ www.hotel-bethel.dk

71 Nyhavn £££ Beautifully restored 200-year-old warehouse. Ancient beams, luxurious suites and some lovely views over the harbour. Good restaurant. ⓐ Nyhavn 71 (Nyhavn area) ❶ 33436200 ⓦ www.71nyhavnhotel.dk

Hotel Fox £££ Individually designed rooms, fabulous buffet breakfast, rooftop terrace and a great lounge with café and bar. ⓐ Jarmers Plads 3 (Around the Three Lakes) ❶ 33133000 ⓦ www.hotelfox.dk

○ *Hotel Alexandra, a design-conscious hotel in a design-conscious city*

Hotel Opera £££ In a quiet street behind Det Kongelige
Teater. Charming, British-inspired with good atmosphere.
ⓐ Tordenskjoldsgade 15 (Nyhavn area) ❶ 33478300
ⓦ www.hotelopera.dk

Ibsens Hotel £££ Converted period building, with rooms built into
the original structures. Free hot drinks and internet in lounge.
ⓐ Vendersgade 23 (Around the Three Lakes) ❶ 33131913
ⓦ www.ibsenshotel.dk

Hotel Maritime £££–£££+ Quiet location close to Nyhavn and the
harbour with small but well-equipped rooms and a pleasant
lounge area. ⓐ Peder Skrams Gade 19 (Nyhavn area) ❶ 33134882
ⓦ www.hotel-maritime.dk

Hotel Alexandra £££+ Design hotel with individually furnished rooms and pieces from several of Denmark's most famous designers. Environmentally friendly, with an allergy-friendly floor and organic breakfast buffet. Adjoining brasserie.
🅰 H C Andersens Boulevard 8 (Rådhuspladsen & the West)
🟠 33744444 🟡 www.hotelalexandra.dk

Radisson SAS Royal Hotel £££+ Skyscraper designed in its entirety by Arne Jacobsen. Amazing views, comfortable rooms and egg chairs.
🅰 Hammerichsgade 1 (Rådhuspladsen & the West) 🟠 33426000
🟡 www.radisson.com

The Square £££+ Located on City Hall square with a view over the city. Stylishly decorated rooms and great breakfast. 🅰 Rådhuspladsen 14 (Rådhuspladsen & the West) 🟠 33381200 🟡 www.thesquare.dk

HOSTELS & SLEEP-INNS

Some hostels have en suite twin rooms, but most are summer-only dormitories. A dormitory bed costs between 100 and 200kr.

City Public Hostel £ Dormitory only, near Central Station. Open 24 hours; bed linen and breakfast extra; free wireless internet access, kitchen and barbeque. ⓐ Absalonsgade 8 (Rådhuspladsen & the West) ⓣ 33312070 ⓦ www.citypublichostel.dk

Sleep-in Green £ Small, ecologically sound hostel open summer only in Nørrebro. ⓐ Ravnsborggade 18 (Around the Three Lakes) ⓣ 35377777 ⓦ www.sleep-in-green.dk

Sleep in Heaven £ Backpacker spot with free internet access and chillout room. ⓐ Struensegade 7 (Around the Three Lakes) ⓣ 35354648 ⓦ www.sleepinheaven.com

Danhostel Copenhagen City £–££ The first designer hostel in Europe offering spotlessly clean and modern dorms and private rooms. ⓐ H C Andersens Boulevard 50 (Rådhuspladsen & the West) ⓣ 33118585 ⓦ www.danhostel.dk

The Danhostel has two sister hostels which offer a similar service: **Copenhagen Downtown** near Studiestræde (ⓐ Vandkunsten 5 ⓣ 7023110 ⓦ www.copenhagendowntown.com), and **Copenhagen Amager**, near the airport (ⓐ Vejlands Allé 200 ⓣ 32522908 ⓦ www.copenhagenyouthhostel.dk).

● *Arne Jacobsen design plus unbeatable views at the Royal Hotel*

THE BEST OF COPENHAGEN

The longer you can spend in Copenhagen, the better. Even when you have sampled the full variety of sights, museums, shops and other delights that the city offers, there's still plenty to see and do in the surrounding area of North Zealand, easily accessible by local train and bus.

A canal cruise is the best way to get an overview of the most picturesque and unique parts of the city. Try **DFDS Canal Tours** (❸ Ticket offices: Gammel Strand 26 & Nyhavn 3 ❶ 32963000 Ⓦ www.canaltours.com ❶ Tours: every half hour 09.15–17.00 mid-Mar–mid-May & Sept–mid-Oct; 09.15–17.30 mid-May–June; 09.15–19.30 July & Aug; every 75 mins 10.00–15.00 mid-Oct–Dec; 10.00–15.00 Sat & Sun only, Jan–mid-Mar).

TOP 10 ATTRACTIONS

- **Tivoli Gardens** An evening of pure fun and pleasure at one of Europe's oldest amusement parks (see page 80)

- **Ny Carlsberg Glyptotek (Carlsberg Sculpture Centre)** Enjoy a coffee in the winter gardens surrounded by stunning sculptures (see page 85)

- **Christiania** A stroll through a unique social experiment (see page 92)

- **Assistens Kirkegård** The most beautiful garden in Copenhagen. Visit Hans Christian Andersen in his place of rest (see page 44)

- **Canal boat cruise** Take a waterborne tour around the city (see opposite)

- *Smørrebrød* Danish speciality, best enjoyed in a traditional city centre café (see page 25)

- **Shopping** in the side streets around Strøget (see page 67)

- **Rosenborg Slot** Admire the crown jewels (see page 108)

- **Vor Frelsers Kirke (Church of Our Saviour)** For the thrill of the climb and the views from the top (see page 98)

- **Roskilde** A trip to see Denmark's old capital and authentic Viking ships (see page 126)

▼ *Detail of a carousel in amusement park Tivoli*

Suggested itineraries

HALF-DAY: COPENHAGEN IN A HURRY

If you're just passing through or snatching some free time on a business trip and only have a morning or an afternoon – where do you go? Art lovers must seek out the Statens Museum for Kunst (National Gallery, see page 112) while pleasure seekers should head straight for the canal tour – sit down and see the lot at the same time, if only from canal level. Anarchists will want to go to Christiania and beer lovers won't go far wrong with a visit to the Carlsberg Visitor Centre.

1 DAY: TIME TO SEE A LITTLE MORE

Start your day with a Danish breakfast – Danish pastries, croissants, black bread and mild Danish cheese and fresh fruit, perhaps in the Radisson (see page 80) where you can simultaneously admire some of Denmark's most famous exports – the egg chair, swan chair and coffee pots by Arne Jacobsen. Fill your morning with one of the half-day suggestions, and maybe your afternoon with one of the others.

Alternatively, stroll over to Strøget, shop your way down to Kongens Nytorv and lunch at Nyhavn, where you can choose one of the Nyhavnside cafés. In the afternoon head down Gothersgade towards Nørreport, where you can while away the time in Kongens Have, the Botanical Gardens or Rosenberg Slot, admiring the crown jewels and wondering why anyone would want cutlery made of glass. Your evening should start with a classy meal, perhaps in the famed restaurant Noma (see page 103), which serves some of the best – and certainly most innovative – Danish cuisine in the city. After dinner, head over to Tivoli for a ride or just wander about catching the performances and the sound and light show.

2–3 DAYS: TIME TO SEE MUCH MORE

With a couple more days Slotsholmen would take up a morning, doing the tour of the royal residence, admiring the Black Diamond and perhaps picnicking in the Royal Library Gardens. The afternoon should be dedicated to some serious culture, perhaps the Statens Museum for Kunst, or the Nationalmuseet (National Museum). Dinner at Custom House (see page 75) followed by a performance at the Opera House, arriving by water taxi, would round off the highbrow evening or you could go on to one of the city's clubs which are just getting started around 01.00. Save your serious shopping for your second or third morning, checking out some of the trendier shops in Nørrebro and Frederiksberg, but spend the afternoon in Christiania, a place like nowhere else. If you like it stay for the evening – there's usually music of some kind going on, or just hang out in a bar. Otherwise one of the canalside restaurants, say Kanalen (page 103) would make a pleasantly romantic evening, followed by a stroll back to the city centre and a late-night bar somewhere behind Illum department store.

LONGER: ENJOYING COPENHAGEN TO THE FULL

On a longer stay you ought to visit some of the smaller art collections, spend an afternoon strolling along the harbour to Amalienborg to see the Queen's winter residence, then on to the Gefion Fountain, the English Church and the Little Mermaid. A week would allow a day trip to Roskilde to visit the Viking Ship Museum and one to Helsingør to see the castle Hamlet never lived in. You could easily while away half a day viewing art and lunching at Louisiana – art in a garden. In the evenings there are movies, the theatre and some good clubs and in between there's always shopping.

Something for nothing

There are lots of things you can do in Copenhagen which are completely free. Most of Copenhagen's museums have free entrance on Wednesdays. All of the churches are free and there are plenty of architectural and design wonders to be seen among them. Be sure to visit Vor Frelsers Kirke in Christianshavn with its beautiful golden spiral steeple. The magnificent **Grundtvigs Kirke** (❸ På Bjerget 14B) just outside the Nørrebro district in Nordvest was designed by the influential lighting and furniture designer Kaare Jensen-Klint, and his father.

Visit the National Library to see late 20th-century cutting-edge design in the form of the Black Diamond (see page 98) and to view the 17th-century architecture of the original library building next door.

All of the parks have a unique layout and offer something special. A less likely place to relax, but one that is well used by joggers, sunbathers and picnickers is the beautiful Assistens Kirkegård, which is in fact a cemetery. As well as some of Denmark's most famous deceased, it contains a wonderful assortment of trees from all around the globe.

There are pleasant walks to be had along the harbour to Kastellet and Den Lille Havfrue (the Little Mermaid), and around Christiania, where you will come across some of the craziest-shaped houses you could ever imagine. Another popular spot to relax is around the Three Lakes. If you want to soak up the atmosphere of Nyhavn, with its expensive canal-side cafés, grab a beer from the supermarket and sit by the canal.

If you are lucky you will find some of the city's free bicycles (see page 57) and you can cycle around the city for nothing but a 20kr returnable deposit.

Sitting on Hans Christian Andersen's lap in Rådhuspladsen for a photo is silly, but everyone does it. You can also wander into the lobby of the Radisson, where everything is designed by Arne Jacobsen, and laze in an egg chair or ask for a tour of room 606 which has been preserved with its original furnishings.

▼ *Visit Thorvaldsens Museet on a Wednesday and get in for nothing*

When it rains

On a rainy day, go and get wet in Rådhuspladsen and look up at the Unibank building on the corner of H C Andersens Boulevard and Vesterbrogade. The whole corner of the building is a giant thermometer topped by a pair of moving statues. When it is sunny a girl on a bicycle moves into view while when it is raining her twin has an umbrella.

All the museums, art galleries, churches, department stores and castles will keep you busy for at least a week of rain. Ny Carlsberg Glyptotek (see page 85) is particularly pleasant in the rain, as you can sit in the conservatory and pretend you are in the tropics. You could spend the whole day in Nationalmuseet (see page 84) and never leave, eating lunch in the café and wandering around the history of the world. Go in without a floor plan and see how long it takes you to find your way out again.

The **Dansk Jødisk Museum** (Museum of Danish Jewish History ⓐ Proviantpassagen 6 ❶ 33112218 Ⓦ www.jewmus.dk) in the Royal Library Gardens is a worthy visit, while the **Tøjhusmuseet** (Royal Arsenal Museum ⓐ Tøjhusgade 3 ❶ 33116037 Ⓦ www.thm.dk) in Slotsholmen is a collection of big and small guns through the ages.

The **House of Amber** (ⓐ Kongens Nytorv 2 ❶ 33116700 Ⓦ www.houseofamber.com ❸ 10.00–18.30 May–Sept; 10.00–17.30 Oct–Apr) has, besides a large supply of amber jewellery and ornaments for you to buy, a museum of amber with chess sets, boxes, ornaments and prehistoric creepy crawlies transfixed for all time.

In Vesterbrogade is **Københavns Bymuseum** (Copenhagen City Museum ⓐ Vesterbrogade 59 ❶ 33210772 Ⓦ www.bymuseum.dk ❸ 10.00–16.00 Thur–Tue, 10.00–21.00 Wed) with a history of the growth of the city and a collection of Søren Kierkegaard's possessions.

● *You're in luck – the Unibank girl says it's going to be sunny*

On arrival

TIME DIFFERENCE
Copenhagen's clocks follow Central European Time (CET). During Daylight Saving Time (end Mar–end Oct), the clocks are put ahead by one hour.

ARRIVING
By air
Copenhagen Kastrup Airport (ⓦ www.cph.dk) is 8 km (5 miles) southeast of the city. A modern and busy airport, there are 24-hour ATMs, exchange facilities (🕒 06.00–22.00), a small general store, post office, car-rental agencies and restaurants. The information desk (🕒 06.00–00.00) will dispense maps and the useful, free *Copenhagen This Week*. It can book hotels for a charge.

The airport is connected to the city centre by rail, metro and bus. The arrivals hall is located in Terminal 3, where you will find a ticket office and ticket machines. Note that the same tickets are valid on all three transport options. A ticket is valid for one hour and costs 33kr at the time of writing.

Trains leave approximately every ten minutes between 04.30 and 00.00, and hourly between 00.00 and 04.30, arriving at Central Station (København H) in 12 minutes, and Nørreport Station in 15–20 minutes. The metro runs at four- to six-minute intervals between 06.00 and 01.00, and at 15- to 20-minute intervals between 01.00 and 06.00. They take 13 minutes to arrive at Kongens Nytorv and 15 minutes to arrive at Nørreport Station.

Buses are the slowest option. Bus 5A runs at 15-minute intervals between 04.30 and 23.30, stopping at Central Station (29 minutes), Rådhuspladsen (33 minutes) and Nørreport Station (37 minutes), before continuing across the Three Lakes through Nørrebro.

If you are staying in the Nyhavn area, take the metro to Kongens Nytorv. If you are staying around the Three Lakes, either take the bus directly there or catch the train or metro to Nørreport, then connect to bus 5A to take you further.

By rail & road

International trains and coaches arrive in Copenhagen at Central Station (Københavns Hovedbanegård, usually called København H). The station concourse has cafés, an internet café, foreign exchange, bike hire, left luggage, showers and an **information centre** (ⓘ 70131415; press 3 for English Ⓦ www.dsb.dk Ⓛ 05.45–23.30).

By water

If you are travelling to Copenhagen by ferry, the arrival point in the city is behind Langelinie (❸ Amerika Plads, Østerbro). Take a short taxi ride to Kongens Nytorv, where you will find a metro stop and several buses.

FINDING YOUR FEET

Copenhagen must be the easiest city in Europe to settle into. The public transport is quick and efficient, everyone speaks better English than you do and will gladly offer assistance and although the currency is unfamiliar it is quickly learned. Many shops show the equivalent price in euros, although few accept them.

The most difficult thing for British visitors will be remembering that the traffic is on the other side of the road and that there are cycle tracks along most roads, fairly distinguishable from pavements. Crossing the street on a red man is breaking the law, so be careful not to get a fine even if the street is empty of cars. You will notice too

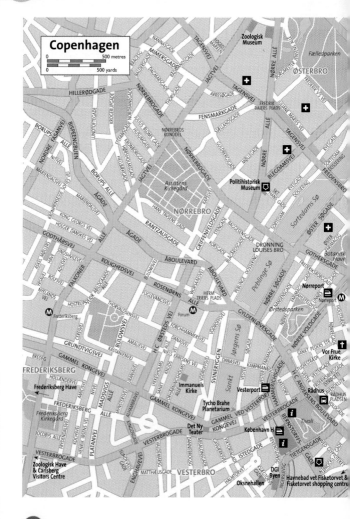

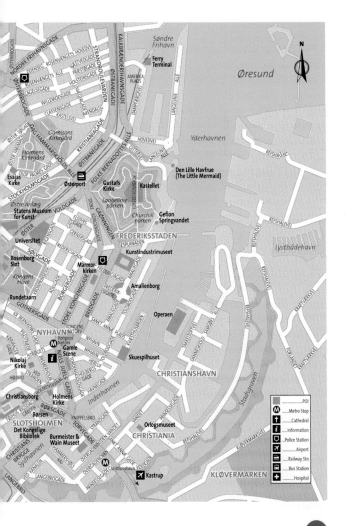

that it is not the custom to hold doors open for the person behind you; a couple of doors in the face will soon make that apparent. Street crime, while not unknown, is certainly rarer than in other European cities, but pickpocketers are on the increase.

ORIENTATION

From Central Station, the city centre stretches northeast, bounded along its southeast edge by the harbour. Directly to the northeast of Central Station across Rådhuspladsen is the long, pedestrianised shopping street Strøget that runs parallel with the harbour all the way to Kongens Nytorv, a second transport hub, and to Nyhavn, where many of the hotels are situated. To the west of Central Station is the other hotel-laden area of Vesterbro. Travelling northwest from Central Station brings you to the Three Lakes area. Just west of the third and fourth lake is the trendy area of Nørrebro. Frederiksberg is west of the first two lakes.

Between Strøget and the harbour is a small island, Slotsholmen, the financial and political heart of the city. East of there is Christianshavn, with its curious community of Christiania. Further south is the island of Amager and the airport.

GETTING AROUND

The **metro system** (❶ 70151615 ⓦ www.m.dk) has two lines, which connect the east and west of the city with the centre, but not with Central Station. Stations you are most likely to use are Nørreport, Kongens Nytorv and Christianshavn. The metro, like the bus service, is zoned and a basic ticket (a little over 20kr) carries you across two zones and can be transferred to a bus journey within those zones within the hour.

The S-train (*S-Tog*) network radiates out from Central Station

IF YOU GET LOST, TRY ...

Excuse me, do you speak English?
Undskyld, taler du engelsk?
Ornskewl, tala do ehng-ehlsg?

How do I get to ...?
Hvordan kommer jeg til ...?
Vohdan komma yai ti ...?

Can you show me on my map?
Kunne du vise mig det på kortet?
Kooneh do veeseh mai di por korrdeht?

along seven separate routes. Destinations and times are shown
in the station concourse and each stop is shown on the platform.
The complete route is displayed electronically so you can check
where you are at any time. Buy a ticket and clip it yourself on the
platform at the start of your journey. Inspectors travel on most
trains and buses and failure to produce a clipped ticket results
in an instant fine.

Buses are boarded at the front, where you pay the driver or clip
your bus card, and exited in the middle. Useful bus routes are:
5A from the airport, via Amager, Slotsholmen and Rådhuspladsen
to Nørrebro
6A from the Zoological Gardens, along Vesterbrogade, to Central
Station, Nørreport Station and across the fourth lake in Østerbro
66 from Central Station to Christianshavn

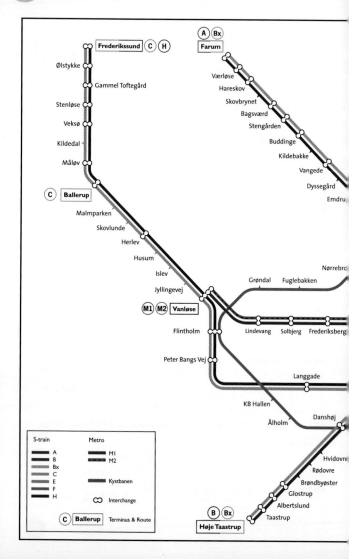

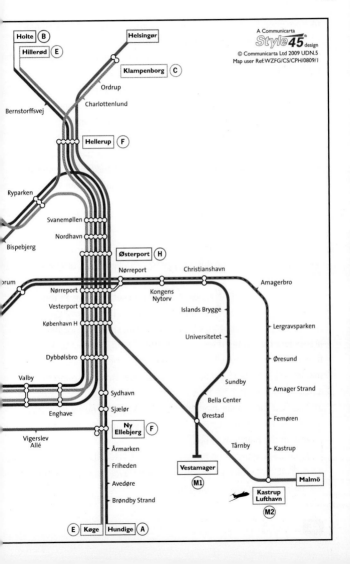

A Communicarta
Style45 design
© Communicarta Ltd 2009 UDN.5
Map user Ref:WZFG/CS/CPH/0809/1

1A from Østerbro to Amelienborg, Nyhavn, the city centre (National Museum, Slotsholmen), Central Station, Fisketorvet and the west **350S** from Dragør to Amager, Christianshavn, Kongens Nytorv, Nørreport, Nørrebro and the northwest.

A particularly useful bus for visitors is the **CityCirkel** (Ⓦ www.citycirkel.dk), which travels around the central zone 1. Buses run every seven minutes or so 09.00–20.00 Monday to Friday, 10.00–16.00 Saturday, and 11.00–15.00 on Sundays and public holidays. There is also a harbour bus with six stops along the harbour: Det Kongelige Bibliotek (The Black Diamond), Knippelsbro (Christianshavn), Nyhavn, Operaen (Opera House), Holmen Nord and Nordre Toldbold (Little Mermaid). The harbour bus runs approximately every 20 minutes 07.00–20.00 Monday to Friday, 10.00–20.00 Saturday, and 10.00–18.30 on Sundays and public holidays.

Single tickets can be bought at the start of each journey in the metro stations or on the bus. *Klippekort*, ten-clip tickets, offer much cheaper journeys and can be bought for two zones (blue), three zones (yellow), up to 'All zones'. A 24-hour ticket covering all zones can also be purchased for approximately 125kr. The zone system is rather complicated, but luckily all of the main sights are located across just two zones. If you travel further afield, it is best to ask how many zones you will need to cover at the ticket office. You can use the *klippekort* or 24-hour ticket to transfer from the metro to a bus (within a one-hour time limit for the *klipperkort*). *Klippekort* and 24-hour tickets are available from kiosks and vending machines at railway and S-train stations. They must be clipped (validated) by you on the platform or bus.

Finally, a useful option for visitors is the CPHCARD (see page 31), a discount card which gives you unlimited travel for 24 or 72 hours and reduced entrance to some sights.

Note that, where public transport options are given in this guide, the most convenient option is listed first followed by the closest alternatives. For further travel advice check Ⓦ www.rejseplanen.dk.

Trishaws, tricycle rickshaws, can be hired around the town and make a green alternative to a conventional taxi. If you prefer to cycle yourself, between April and September the city operates a system of free bicycle use. At 125 stands around the city centre are racks where a free bike can be removed by inserting a 20kr coin. The bikes have solid wheels with adverts on them and no gears. If your trip is in late August do not count on finding one. Bikes can also be rented from one of the many bike shops around the city for about 70kr a day.

Bicycles can be carried on S-trains and the metro in designated carriages (usually the end carriages), and are easily parked – back

● *Try one of Copenhagen's eco-friendly taxis*

wheel first on the S-train. You are, however, not allowed to embark or disembark at Nørreport Station with your bike during rush hour (07.00–08.30 and 15.30–17.00). Bikes are not allowed on buses. Some rules of the road should be noted: bus passengers often alight onto the cycle path and cyclists must give way; cyclists may not turn left at major road junctions – they have to dismount and cross at the pedestrian crossing; stay on the right side of the cycle path; cyclists are allowed to overtake one another; when you decide to stop you should raise your right hand (do a 'how' sign) to signal to those behind you.

Getting around the city by car is manageable, although the city centre itself is better done on foot or by bike. Parking is difficult and expensive, except on Sundays and public holidays, when it is free. Cars drive on the right. Car hire is easy and most hire companies do not require an international driving licence. To park you need a ticket, available from roadside machines, which you display inside the windscreen. The city is divided into zones with the more remote areas costing less to park in. If you are unsure of the zone and requirements, ask a local as a fine of over 500kr will be administered if you get it wrong.

CAR HIRE
The following companies also have booths at the airport.
Avis ⓐ Sluseholmen 3 ⓣ 33268080 ⓦ www.avis.dk
Budget ⓐ Vester Farimagsgade 7 ⓣ 33557000 ⓦ www.budget.dk
Europcar ⓐ Gammel Kongevej 13 ⓣ 70113355 ⓦ www.europcar.dk
Hertz ⓐ Ved Vesterport 3 ⓣ 33179020 ⓦ www.hertzdk.dk

Ⓓ *Copenhagen's Nyhavn in spring*

THE CITY OF
Copenhagen

Nyhavn area

This is the epicentre of tourist Copenhagen. The broad pedestrianised shopping street called Strøget starts here with Kongens Nytorv (King's Square) at its head. To the east is Nyhavn (New Harbour), the short canal that once welcomed trading ships but which now houses a multitude of open-air restaurants, stylish hotels and swanky yachts. A short walk from here takes you to Amalienborg Slot (Amalienborg Palace), still lived in by the Royal Family but open to the public, where you can watch the changing of the guard. Further north along the harbour an old fortress, churches, gardens, museums, the photogenic Gefion Springvandet (Gefion Fountain) and the Little Mermaid – an overrated but essential stop on your itinerary – are all strung together along a harbourside walk with views over to the new Opera House and Christianshavn.

SIGHTS & ATTRACTIONS

Amalienborg Slot (Amalienborg Palace)

The four palaces which make up Amalienborg, one of which is still lived in by the Queen of Denmark, were designed by the architect Nicolai Eigtved as homes for four of the city's wealthiest burghers but were commandeered by the Royals after their own palace in Slotsholmen burned down. Architecturally tasteful rather than stunning, the courtyard buzzes with tourists snapping away. For a good laugh, don't miss the changing of the guard. A photogenic fountain fronts the courtyard but the real draw is Levetzau Palace, or Christian VIII's Palace, now a museum called The Royal Danish Collection, Amalienborg. It depicts the life and times of the Glücksburger dynasty, and is a storage facility for the Queen's library. ⓐ Amalienborg Plads ⓣ 33122186

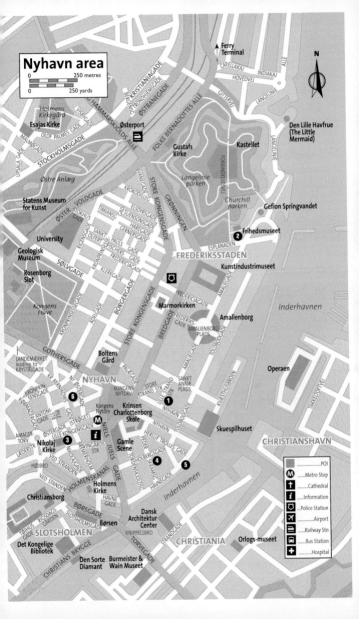

Ⓦ www.kongehuset.dk Ⓛ 10.00–16.00 May–Oct; 11.00–16.00
Tues–Sun, Nov–Apr; guided tours in English: 13.00 & 14.30 Sat
& Sun Ⓝ Bus: 1A, 6A, 15, 350S; CityCirkel: Skt Annæ Plads;
metro: Kongens Nytorv. Admission charge

Frederiksstaden

To the north of Nyhavn, Frederiksstaden is a grand building project
laid out by Frederik V in the 18th century in celebration of the 300th
anniversary of the House of Oldenburg. Its wide boulevards and
French-influenced architecture were commissioned by various royal
hangers-on to designs by the architect Nicolai Eigtved. At its centre

🔻 *All roads lead to busy Kongens Nytorv*

is Bredgade, full of classy boutiques and auction houses, and the pretty square of Sankt Annæ Plads, with its church Garnisonskirken.

⊙ CityCirkel: Skt Annæ Plads

Gefion Springvandet (Gefion Fountain)

A walk along the harbour towards Langelinie on a sunny day is a treat in itself with the new Opera House on the opposite bank, the tour boats chugging past and, best of all, no pedestrian crossings or cyclists. At its northern end is the Gefion Fountain. It was inaugurated in 1908, sponsored by Carlsberg and designed by Anders Bundegård. The fountain tells the story of the goddess Gefion, who, offered as much land as she could plough in a night, turned her sons into oxen

and created Danish Zealand. It is set in attractive parkland beside St Alban's Church (also known as the English Church), and creates some fascinating effects of light on water. ❸ Amaliegade ⓝ Bus: 1A, 15, 26; S-train: Østerport

Kongens Nytorv (King's Square)

If you want to get your bearings in Copenhagen this is the place to start. Three main streets, Bredgade, Nyhavn and Strøget, radiate out from it and it forms a hub for journeys by metro and bus. The square itself, a huge cobbled garden with traffic roaring around it, comes alive in winter when an artificial ice rink is set up and during the summer often displays photographic and art exhibitions.

Around the square are some elegant buildings. **Det Kongelige Teater** (The Royal Theatre ❸ Kongens Nytorv ❶ 33696933 ⓦ www.kglteater.dk) was, before the opening of the new Opera House and playhouse, a major cultural centre, staging ballet, opera and dramatic performances in its two auditoria. Although now usually referred to as Gamle Scene ('Old Stage'), it retains its grandeur and continues to host a busy programme of ballet and theatre productions. The building is fairly recent, dating from 1872, but a theatre has been on this site since 1748. The statues which grace the exterior are some of the big names associated with the theatre's founding and it is worth wandering through the arch across Tordenskjoldsgade to admire the arch's ceiling frescoes.

Carrying on clockwise round the square brings you to Magasin du Nord, once the Hotel du Nord and now a classy department store. Hans Christian Andersen fans can wander up to the third floor, where the room he lived in for a time is open to the public.

▶ *The Royal Guard at Amalienborg*

DEN LILLE HAVFRUE (THE LITTLE MERMAID)

One of the most frequently mutilated pieces of statuary in northern Europe, this diminutive creature has been beheaded on several occasions, lost limbs and suffered several other attacks of vandalism. It was commissioned in 1909 by beer magnate Carl Jacobsen (founder of Carlsberg) after watching an opera of the story by Hans Christian Andersen. More interesting is the daily circus around the statue, with hordes of tourists climbing out on to the rocks to have their photos taken and the tour boats lined up to pull in close for a better view. It's one of those things you just have to do. 🚇 Langelinie 🚌 Bus: 1A, 15, 26; harbour bus: Nordre Toldbold; S-train: Østerport

Further clockwise again brings you to the 5-star Hotel d'Angleterre, another grand 18th-century building, where for not a small amount you can enjoy afternoon tea. The hotel always decorates its façade elaborately at Christmas time. 🚌 Bus 1A, 15, 350S; CityCirkel/metro: Kongens Nytorv

Marmorkirken (Marble Church)

On the opposite side of Bredgade from Amelienborg Slot is Frederiks Kirke, more popularly known as Marmorkirken. This grand church was in fact intended to be much more elaborate than it is, but due to financial problems, among other things, the church was built to its present (still very impressive) form between 1749 and 1894. The interior is not quite as dramatic as the exterior and was never intended to be. The real thrill of a visit to the church is not so much the interior as the trip to the top of the dome, which gives amazing views over the city. The journey upwards involves a tour guide, scrambling between the inner and outer roof domes and climbing through a trapdoor, but it is well worth the trip. Take note of the opening times and avoid wedding days, when the church is closed to the public. ⓐ Frederiksgade 4 ⓣ 33150144 ⓦ www.marmorkirken.dk ⓛ 10.00–17.00 Mon, Tues, Thur & Sat, 10.00–18.30 Wed, 12.00–17.00 Fri & Sun; dome tour: 13.00 & 15.00 mid-June–Aug; 13.00 & 15.00 Sat & Sun only, Sept–mid-June ⓝ CityCirkel: St. Kongensgadev. Admission charge for dome

Nyhavn (New Harbour)

Built in 1671 to bring ships into the centre of the city, the little canal has been gentrified in the last 30 years from a pretty sleazy docks area to a quaint, colourful, village-style place. The low-rise multicoloured buildings were once the homes and workplaces of merchants. In the 19th century three of these buildings (nos. 20, 67 and 18) were home to Hans Christian Andersen, while the street itself became a red-light district. Today Nyhavn buzzes in summer with restaurants and the pavement is swathed in tables and chairs. ⓝ Bus: 1A, 15, 350S; CityCirkel/harbour bus: Nyhavn; metro: Kongens Nytorv

Upper Strøget

From Kongens Nytorv the long pedestrianised shopping street of Strøget begins at Østergade with all of the high-end fashion stores. This street will become familiar as your time in Copenhagen passes – it's difficult to walk down it without being drawn into its department stores, or sitting down to people-watch in one of its pavement cafés. Along here is the **Guinness World Record Museum** (ⓐ Ostergade 16 ⓣ 33368101 ⓛ 09.30–21.30 mid-June–Aug; 10.00–18.00 Sept–mid-June. Admission charge).

For free entertainment, simply check out the many human statues, string quarters and trinket-sellers. CityCirkel: Høbroplads

CULTURE

Frihedsmuseet (Museum of Danish Resistance)

This purpose-built museum chronologically tells the story of the years of German occupation which Denmark suffered during World War II, their belated but increasing resistance to the occupation, the sacrifices of those brave enough to stand against Nazism, and their amazing decision in 1943 to ferry their Jewish population away to neutral Sweden in a succession of small boats in defiance of the Nazi orders for deportation to the death camps. In the grounds, open to the public in the summer months, is an underground shelter used during the war. Particularly poignant are the letters written to their families by resistance members who were executed for their efforts. 🄰 Churchillparken 7 🄸 33473921 🄦 www.frihedsmuseet.dk 🄻 10.00–17.00 Tues–Sun, May–Sept; 10.00–15.00 Tues–Sun, Oct–Apr 🄽 Bus: 1A, 15, 19, 26; harbour bus: Nordre Toldbold; S-train: Østerport

Kunstindustrimuseet (Danish Museum of Art & Design)

Housed in what was once the Frederiks Hospital, part of the great 18th-century development of Frederiksstaden, this collection, funded by the Carlsberg Foundation, contains over 300,000 items of furniture, ceramics, silver, textiles, carpets and more. A changing series of exhibitions is produced alongside the permanent collection. There is an excellent section of crafts from Asia, lots of Danish design – chairs especially – and the exhibitions are organised into time periods, so that you get a sense of the way design has changed over the centuries. The excellent café is

⬥ *The dramatic Gefion Fountain*

furnished with lovely tables and chairs and the courtyard is an excellent place to rest tired feet after a good wander around. In the courtyard there is a plaque commemorating the life of the philosopher Kierkegaard, who died in the hospital in 1855. ⓐ Bredgade 68 ⓘ 33185656 ⓦ www.kunstindustrimuseet.dk ⏰ 11.00–17.00 Tues–Sun 🚌 Bus: 1A, 15; CityCirkel: Skt Annæ Plads; S-train: Østerport; metro: Kongens Nytorv. Admission charge (free Wed)

Skuespilhuset (Playhouse)

The impressive Skuespilhuset theatre was completed in 2008, after Danish architects Boje Lundgaard and Lene Tranberg won a prestigious international competition for its design (see page 18). Situated at the opposite end of Nyhavn directly overlooking the harbour, the Playhouse can house up to 650 guests in its three auditoria and has excellent facilities for visitors, including people with disabilities or hearing impairments. Its busy programme of drama, musical and dance productions is second to none. The café and restaurant Ofelia is open both to theatre guests and the general public throughout the week (from 10.00 until the final curtain falls) and is so popular that you're strongly advised to book: there are dinner seatings at 17.00–17.45 and 19.45–20.00. Ofelia has fantastic views over the harbour and a huge outdoor harbourside terrace and cocktail bar, weather permitting. ⓐ Sankt Annæ Plads 36 ❶ 33696933 Ⓦ www.skuespilhus.dk ❻ Box office: 10.00–23.30 Mon–Sat, during performances only Sun Ⓝ Bus: 1A, 29, 350S; CityCirkel: Kvæsthusgade; harbour bus: Nyhavn; metro: Kongens Nytorv

RETAIL THERAPY

Here is the heart of shopping paradise. Visit the pedestrianised, café-lined street Strøget, its satellite streets Købmagergade, Kronprinsensgade and Læderstræde, and the smart stores around Kongens Nytorv. The two big department stores Illum and Magasin du Nord are handy.

Georg Jensen Everything you could ever want in silver. Worth going in just to admire the pieces. ⓐ Amagertorv 4 ❶ 33114080 Ⓦ www.georgjensen.dk ❻ 10.00–19.00 Mon–Fri, 10.00–17.00 Sat,

⬤ *Amalienborg Palace, the royal winter residence*

12.00–16.00 Sun, June–Aug; 10.00–18.00 Mon–Fri, 10.00–17.00 Sat, Sept–May Ⓐ Bus 1A, 15, 350S; CityCirkel: Højbro Plads; metro: Kongens Nytorv

Illums Bolighus A small, busy department store selling beautiful designer objects for the house and home, as well as gifts, jewellery and clothing. Ⓐ Amagertorv 10 Ⓣ 33141941 Ⓦ www.illumsbolighus.dk Ⓛ 10.00–18.00 Mon–Thur, 10.00–19.00 Fri, 10.00–17.00 Sat Ⓝ Bus: 1A, 15, 350S; CityCirkel: Højbro Plads; metro: Kongens Nytorv

Mads Nørgaard An institution in Copenhagen, selling Danish and international designer clothing for men and women. Ⓐ Amagertorv 15 Ⓣ 33320128 Ⓦ www.madsnorgaard.com Ⓛ 10.00–18.00 Mon–Thur, 10.00–19.00 Fri, 10.00–17.00 Sat Ⓝ Bus 1A, 15, 350S; CityCirkel: Højbro Plads; metro: Kongens Nytorv

Royal Copenhagen Dedicated to the revered, over 200-year-old royal porcelain. Has a small seconds store. Ⓐ Amagertorv 6 Ⓣ 33137181 Ⓦ www.royalcopenhagen.com Ⓛ 10.00–18.00 Mon–Thur, 10.00–19.00 Fri, 10.00–17.00 Sat, Oct–May; 10.00–19.00 Mon–Fri, 10.00–17.00 Sat, 12.00–17.00 Sun, June–Sept Ⓝ Bus 1A, 15, 350S; CityCirkel: Højbro Plads; metro: Kongens Nytorv

Søstrene Grene Denmark's first discount store, selling everything from children's toys to crockery, tea and art equipment. Ⓐ Amagertorv 29 Ⓦ www.grenes.dk Ⓛ 10.00–18.00 Mon–Thur, 10.00–19.00 Fri, 10.00–17.00 Sat Ⓝ Bus 1A, 15, 350S; CityCirkel: Højbro Plads; metro: Kongens Nytorv

TAKING A BREAK

The obvious place for a coffee or lunch in the area is Nyhavn, where in summer tables litter the waterside and you are spoilt for choice. Back in Strøget the department stores have cool underground coffee shops or you can sit out on the street and people-watch.

Hyttefadet £ ❶ A traditional Danish restaurant – perfect for trying *smørrebrød*. Warm, welcoming, friendly service and occasionally live music in the evenings. ⓐ Nyhavn 25 ❶ 33120107 ⓦ www.hyttefadet.dk ⓛ 09.00–01.00 Sun–Thur, 09.00–02.00 Fri & Sat ⓝ Bus: 350S, 1A, 15; CityCirkel/harbour bus: Nyhavn; metro: Kongens Nytorv

Sommerhuset £–££ ❷ Garden café and restaurant set in a peaceful area by the Gefion Fountain. Danish specialities, a barbeque in the evenings and an extensive organic wine list. ⓐ Churchillparken 7 ❶ 33321314 ⓛ 09.00–00.00 May–Oct ⓝ Bus: 350S, 1A, 15, 26; harbour bus: Nordre Toldbold; S-train: Østerport

Caféen i Nikolaj ££ ❸ Housed in Nikolaj Kirke (Nikolaj Church), with charming indoor seating and a large terrace area. ⓐ Nikolaj Plads 12 ❶ 33116313 ⓦ www.nikolajkirken.dk ⓛ 11.30–23.00 Mon–Sat, July, Aug & Dec; 11.30–17.00 Mon–Sat, Jan–June & Sept–Nov ⓝ Bus: 6A, 1A, 15, 26; CityCirkel: Højbro Plads; metro: Kongens Nytorv

AFTER DARK

Enjoy the early evening at any of the numerous bars in Nyhavn or in the streets between Upper Strøget and Købmagergade.

○ *Enjoy a harbourside meal at Custom House*

RESTAURANTS

Fuego £ ❹ Argentinian restaurant, brasserie and wine bar offering European cuisine. 'Eat, drink and dance' is the motto at weekends. ⓐ Holbergsgade 14 ❶ 33131171 ⓦ www.fuego.dk ❶ 18.00–01.00 Mon–Thur, 18.00–03.00 Fri & Sat (kitchen closes 22.00) ⓝ Bus: 350S, 1A, 15; CityCirkel: Højbro Plads; metro: Kongens Nytorv

Custom House ££–£££ ❺ This beautiful old customs building has been transformed by Terence Conran into three stylish, top calibre restaurants: Bacino (Italian), Bar&Grill (brasserie) and Ebisu (Japanese). There is even a deli. ⓐ Havnegade 44 ❶ 33310130 ⓦ www.customhouse.dk ❶ 11.30–00.00 Mon–Wed, 11.30–01.00 Thur, 11.30–02.00 Fri & Sat, 11.00–00.00 Sun ⓝ Bus: 350S, 1A, 15; CityCirkel: Kvæsthusgade; harbour bus: Nyhavn

L'Alsace £££ ❻ French restaurant, with foie gras and seafood a speciality. Pretty courtyard outdoor seating in summer. ⓐ Ny Østergade 9 ❶ 33145743 ⓦ www.alsace.dk ❶ 11.30–00.00 Mon–Sat ⓝ Bus: 350S, 1A, 15; CityCirkel: Højbro Plads; metro: Kongens Nytorv

BARS & CLUBS

Boltens Gaard Home to several of Copenhagen's clubs and bars. ⓐ Behind Gothersgade 8 ⓝ Bus: 350S, 1A, 15; CityCirkel/harbour bus: Nyhavn; metro: Kongens Nytorv

Culture Box Drink a cocktail in the neighbouring Cocktail Box before heading to Culture Box, one of Copenhagen's most popular nightclubs. ⓐ Kronprinsessegade 54A ❶ 33325050 ⓦ www.culture-box.com ❶ 00.00–06.00 Thur–Sat ⓝ Bus 350S; CityCirkel: Kongens Have

Rådhuspladsen & the West

Rådhuspladsen (City Hall Square) is a large, pedestrianised area overshadowed by the grand City Hall. The square is one of the major hubs of the city. Early in the morning it bustles with people on their way to work, tables and chairs are drawn up into close huddles, and traffic roars across the huge road junctions that surround it. But later a sunny piazza emerges: coffee shops, hot dog stands, trinkets laid out on the ground, herds of tourists and shoppers heading for the southern end of Strøget, the long shopping street that leads to Kongens Nytorv. At night the surrounding buildings disappear to be replaced by disembodied blinking neon and the fairy lights of Tivoli.

Radiating out from the square is a fascinating series of contrasting tourist attractions, including the Dansk Design Center, Tivoli, the Ny Carlsberg Glyptotek, the grandiose Palace Hotel and Ripley's Believe It or Not Museum. Lording over it all is Copenhagen's most famous immigrant, Hans Christian Andersen, whose statue sits close to the boulevard named after him.

SIGHTS & ATTRACTIONS

Carlsberg Visitors Centre

The Visitors Centre, in a brewing house built at the turn of the 20th century, displays the history of brewing and of the Carlsberg Brewery, which you can smell but not see. Unfortunately the free beer on your tour has been stopped, but you still have the opportunity to buy one. ❸ Gamle Carlsberg Vej 11 ❶ 33271282 ⓦ www.visitcarlsberg.dk ❺ 10.00–17.00 Tues, Wed & Fri–Sun, 10.00–19.30 Thur ❷ Bus: 6A, 18, 26; S-train: Enghave. Admission charge

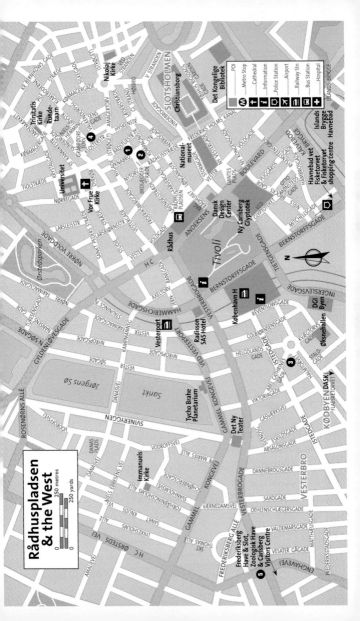

Frederiksberg Have & Slot (Frederiksberg Park & Palace)

Huge, pleasant park littered with attractions. You could spend an afternoon out here visiting the sights, and the park makes a lovely break in between visits. On the south side is a museum of modern glass, the Cisterne. In the southeast corner is the Royal Danish Horticulture Garden, used in summer for outdoor concerts, while the Spa Room holds regular exhibitions and concerts. Beside the Horticulture Garden is the summer palace Frederiksberg Slot, which although not open to the public, is well worth admiring for its 18th-century Italianate style. Copenhagen Zoo (see page 83) backs onto the park, and visitors have the pleasure of seeing elephants basking in the sun in the elephant enclosure without having to pay to enter the zoo. Look out for the *Suttetræ* (dummy tree), on which growing children hang their old dummies as a farewell ritual.

Frederiksberg Have 🕐 06.00–17.00, 18.00 or 19.00 Oct–Mar; 06.00–21.00 or 22.00 Apr–Sept (hours vary) 🚍 Bus: 18, 6A

Cisterne Museet for Moderne Glaskunst 🅰 Søndermarken 🕐 33219310 🌐 www.cisternerne.dk 🕐 14.00–18.00 Thur & Fri, 11.00–17.00 Sat & Sun 🚍 Bus: 18, 6A. Admission charge

Lower Strøget

Joining on from the smarter Upper Strøget (see page 67), this series of linked pedestrianised streets – Frederiksberggade, Nygade, Amagertorv and Østergade – is always teeming with buskers and pavement sellers displaying their wares on the ground. At the junction with Nørregade are Gammeltorv and Nytorv (Old Square and New Square), with their centrepieces the Domhuset (Courthouse) and Caritas Fountain (1608). 🚍 CityCirkel: Rådhuspladsen or Gammeltorv

Rådhus (City Hall)

Rådhus was completed in 1905, the work of Danish architect Martin Nyrop. Look closely at the exterior and you will see a multitude of odd figures from gargoyle water spouts to fierce dragons guarding

🔺 *Frederik VI welcomes you to Frederiksberg Have*

the entrance. You are free to wander about the equally ornate interior but a guided tour would make more sense of what you are seeing.

Take a look at the Jens Olsen's World Clock just inside the main entrance, with its 570,000-year calendar. The multitude of shivering dials tell stunningly accurate time as well as plotting assorted planetary orbits and lunar and solar eclipses.

A tour of the bell tower involves 300 steps then a scramble to the spire, but there are some great views towards Kongens Nytorv. The building has a pretty enclosed garden which is good for a quiet break. ⓐ Rådhuspladsen 1 ⓣ 33663366 ⓛ 07.45–17.00 Mon–Fri, 09.30–13.00 Sat; guided tours in English (minimum 4 people): 15.00 Mon–Fri, 10.00 & 11.00 Sat ⓜ CityCirkel: Rådhuspladsen. Admission charge for clock, tower and tours

Radisson SAS Hotel

Designed by Arne Jacobsen in 1960. IIf you don't stay here you can always lounge about the lobby or have a drink in the bar, admiring the crazy 1960s steel light fittings or swinging about in the Jacobsen egg and swan chairs. One of the rooms (606) has been preserved in its original style. In a case by the lifts are some of Jacobsen's designs, many of which you can buy over the road in the design shop. ⓐ Hammerichsgade 1 ⓣ 33426000 ⓦ www.radisson.com ⓜ CityCirkel/S-train: Vesterport or København H

Tivoli

One of the oldest amusement parks in Europe, Tivoli is also one of Copenhagen's top tourist attractions. As darkness falls and the fairy lights hover over your head, the bandstands fill with music and the rides start to whirl. You will feel like you are ten years old

The lower end of Strøget offers plenty of free entertainment

again, just for a while. Save Tivoli for a warm night and enjoy a meal that will coincide with the nightly performances – programmes are posted up outside. Don't miss the sound and light show, on 30 minutes before the gardens close. Every Friday evening during the summer season a free concert, Friday Rock, is put on for visitors at 22.00 (entrance fee to Tivoli still applies). On special occasions, such as Tivoli's official birthday on 15 August, there are fireworks displays.

The daytime is for real children and gardeners. There are over 30 rides, pantomime performances, sticky things to eat and fairground stalls. Gardeners will admire the planting; someone with a real eye for design fills the beds. Beautiful weeping willows, linden and elm trees provide a backdrop to the nightly sound and light show and there isn't a municipal shrub to be seen. ❸ Vesterbrogade 3 ❶ 33151001 ❿ www.tivoli.dk ❹ 11.00–23.00 Sun–Thur, 11.00–00.30 Fri, 11.00–00.00 Sat, mid-Apr–mid-June & mid-Aug–mid-Sept; 11.00–00.00 Sun–Thur, 11.00–00.30 Fri & Sat, mid-June–mid-Aug; 11.00–22.00 Sun–Thur, 11.00–23.00 Fri & Sat, late Nov–23 Dec; see website for opening times around Halloween; closed other periods of year ❽ Bus: 1A, 2A, 5A, 6A; CityCirkel/S-train: København H. Admission charge and charges for rides and some shows

Tycho Brahe Planetarium
IMAX theatre that uses state-of-the-art technology to display the night skies, as well as showing stomach-churning movies. The planetarium is named after the great Danish astronomer Tycho Brahe (1546–1601) who discovered the constellation Cassiopeia (the Big Dipper). ❸ Gammel Kongevej 10, corner of Vester Søgade at bottom of lakes ❶ 33121224 ❿ www.tycho.dk ❹ 09.30–21.00 Tues–Sun, 13.00–21.00 Mon ❽ CityCirkel/S-train: Vesterport. Admission charge

Vesterbro

For a long time the part of the city which tourists first encounter – Central Station and many of the city's middle-range hotels are here, as was the red-light district – Vesterbro has become less obtrusive lately. There are still some sex shops, though, and a few junkies and alcoholics still congregate at the back of the station. As Vesterbrogade heads out west towards Frederiksberg the streets take on a decidedly more local atmosphere, with lots of small ethnic restaurants and take-aways from the Asian and Turkish immigrants who have settled in the area. Carry on further and as you near Frederiksberg Park you enter net-curtained leafy suburbs where trendy designer boutiques, cafés, and fine-dining restaurants replace the fast-food outlets and cheap shops.

Zoologisk Have (Zoological Gardens)

Founded in 1859, this is one of Europe's oldest zoos. Although small by the standards of others, it provides comfortable accommodation for its captive animals. There is a children's section containing native farm animals, separate sections for animals from the South American pampas and from the African savannah and an enclosure designed by Norman Foster for the zoo's three new elephants, a gift from the King of Thailand. Climb the 40 m (130 ft) tower for great views across the city. ⓐ Roskildevej 32 ⓣ 70200200 ⓦ www.zoo.dk ⓛ 09.00–16.00, 17.00 or 18.00 Sept–late June (times vary); 09.00–21.00 late June–Aug ⓥ Bus: 6A, 4A. Admission charge

CULTURE

Kødbyen

A short walk past Øksnehallen down Halmtorvet brings you to

the old wholesale food district, which literally translates as 'meat town'. Many of the empty shops and offices have now been filled by graphic designers, architects and designers, transforming into a hub of creativity and innovation – even one of the mainstream TV channels has moved its headquarters here. In particular, don't miss the alternative photo gallery **DASK** (ⓐ Flæsketorvet 24 ⓣ 60708149 ⓛ 12.00–18.00 Wed–Fri, 12.00–16.00 Sat). ⓐ Flæsketorvet, behind Halmtorvet ⓦ www.koedbyen.kk.dk ⓝ Bus 1A, 5A, 250S; S-train: Dybbølsbro or København H; CityCirkel: København H

Nationalmuseet (National Museum)

Seeing everything in this museum in one day would be exhausting. A word of warning before you begin: get a plan of the exhibitions before you set out.

The Danish early history section comes mainly from Denmark's many bogs and fields – Viking helmets and *luren* (Bronze Age musical instruments), jewellery and weapons, a first-century chariot from Jutland, excavated Bronze Age graves, and the superb Trundholm Sun Chariot – a bronze model of the chariot of the sun god pulling the sun across the sky.

The upper floors continue the history of Denmark in medieval and Renaissance times, with the largely ecclesiastical and royal exhibits glistening with gold and jewels.

The ethnographic section is strong on Inuit culture, with sculptures, clothing, amulets and reams of whalebone, kayaks and harpoons. Other sections of the museum are dedicated to classical antiquities, including an exceptional collection of black- and red-figure Greek pottery.

A children's museum packs all of these exhibits into a few experiences. Here you can play in the shop from Pakistan, pretend

DANSK DESIGN CENTER

This purpose-built showcase of Danish design holds
a changing set of design exhibits, and the basement has
a permanent collection of iconic items, such as wonderbras,
tetrapaks, Jacobsen coffee pots and Dyson vacuum cleaners.
An excellent shop sells collapsible travel gear. ➋ H C Andersens
Boulevard 27 ➊ 33693369 ➍ www.ddc.dk ➌ 10.00–17.00 Mon,
Tues, Thur & Fri, 10.00–21.00 Wed, 11.00–16.00 Sat & Sun
➍ Bus: 2A, 5A, 6A, 250S. Admission charge (free from 17.00 Wed)

to sail in a Viking ship, fire crossbows and sit inside a Tuareg tent.
A section dedicated to coins and an annex called the Victorian
Home (visit by guided tour only) plus a windmill from Christianshavn
make up the rest of the collection. ➋ Ny Vestergade 10 ➊ 33134411
➍ www.nationalmuseet.dk ➌ 10.00–17.00 Tues–Sun ➍ Bus: 1A, 2A,
5A; CityCirkel: Nationalmuseet or Ny Vestergade

Ny Carlsberg Glyptotek (Carlsberg Sculpture Centre)

This astonishing art collection, mostly donated by beer baron Carl
Jacobsen, needs at least a day to do it justice. If you can't spare that,
you should decide if the French collection or the Mediterranean
antiquities interest you most and focus on your art of choice.

The museum was built in 1897 around the beautiful Winter
Garden, a conservatory filled with tropical plants and statues.
The earlier collection donated by Jacobsen consists of hundreds
of ancient artefacts tracing the history of sculpture from ancient
Sumerian, through Egyptian, Phoenician to Greek, including a huge
collection of Etruscan and ancient Greek items. The more modern

French wing includes a collection of paintings by former Copenhagen resident Paul Gauguin, which were donated to the city by Jacobsen's son Helge. To this collection has been added works by Corot, Renoir, Monet, Pisarro, Cézanne, Toulouse-Lautrec and Van Gogh. Danish art is well represented here too. The Winter Garden has an excellent café where you can eat your Danish among the palm trees to the sound of the Water Mother with Children fountain. ⊕ Dantes Plads 7 ⊕ 33418141 ⊕ www.glyptoteket.dk ⊕ 11.00–17.00 Tues–Sun; tours in English: 14.00 Wed ⊕ Bus: 2A, 5A, 6A; CityCirkel: Ny Carlsberg Glyptotek. Admission charge (free Sun)

Øksnehallen

This beautiful building was originally where oxen and cows stood in line before being sent to the slaughter house. It is now a huge exhibition and culture centre hosting many of Copenhagen's major events. All the buildings surrounding the hall have also maintained their original exterior and now house a variety of art houses, youth centres and laid-back cafés playing live music at the weekends. ⊕ Halmtorvet 11 ⊕ 33860400 ⊕ www.oeksnehallen.dk ⊕ 11.00–18.00 depending on the exhibition ⊕ Bus: 1A; S-train/CityCirkel: København H

RETAIL THERAPY

Birna Fashion concept store created by an Icelandic designer. Good design, quality, practicality and individuality. ⊕ Istedgade 99 ⊕ 33257913 ⊕ www.birna.net ⊕ 11.00–18.00 Mon–Thur, 11.00–19.00 Fri, 11.00–16.00 Sat ⊕ Bus: 10; CityCirkel/S-train: København H

Fisketorvet The perfect option for shopping if the weather is not too great. This indoor harbourside shopping centre has a good range of clothing, shoe and gift shops, as well as several nice cafés. 🅰 Kalvebod Brygge 59 ☎ 33366400 🌐 www.fisketorvet.dk 🕐 10.00–20.00 Mon–Fri, 10.00–17.00 Sat 🚌 Bus 1A; S-train: Dybbølsbro

Ichinen Famed for its crazy t-shirt designs and prints and for its designer lamp shades. You can also find unique gifts and homeware here. 🅰 Istedgade 59 ☎ 33794717 🕐 11.00–18.00 Mon–Fri, 10.00–15.00 Sat 🚌 Bus: 10; CityCirkel/S-train: København H

The Latin Quarter Sandwiched between Nørre Voldgade and Lower Strøget is the trendy Latin Quarter, which is littered with alternative shops selling men's and women's fashion, accessories and music. There are also several good second-hand stores – look out for **København K (KBHK)** 🅰 Studiestræde 32b ☎ 33330889 🕐 11.00–18.00 Mon–Thur, 11.00–19.00 Fri, 11.00–15.00 Sat 🚌 Bus: 5A, 6A; CityCirkel: Rådhuspladsen or Gammeltorv

Saint Tropez One of Denmark's leading designer chain stores with locations in Germany, Sweden and Ireland, selling Saint Tropez fashion designs for women. Lower prices than boutique designers, but good quality clothing and accessories. 🅰 Vesterbrogade 41 ☎ 33310017 🌐 www.sainttropez.com 🕐 10.00–18.00 Mon–Thur, 10.00–19.00 Fri, 10.00–16.00 Sat 🚌 Bus: 6A

TAKING A BREAK

From Rådhuspladsen, wander down Farvergade and Kompagnistræde, which are lined with numerous cafés and restaurants. Turn left towards Gråbrødretorv, a quaint 18th-century square circled with cafés and restaurants. Towards Veserbro, there is no shortage of options at Halmtorvet, the side streets off Vesterbrogade and along Istedgade.

Café Sorgenfri £ ❶ 'No Worries Café'. Traditional Danish lunch in museum-like surroundings. ⓐ Brolæggerstræde 8 ❶ 33115880 ⓦ www.cafesorgenfri.dk ⏱ 11.00–23.00 (kitchen closes 20.45) Mon–Sat, 12.00–18.00 (kitchen closes 17.00) Sun ⓝ Bus 6A; CityCirkel: Nationalmuseet or Stormbroen

Rizraz £ ❷ Vegetarian all-day buffet with a Mediterranean twist, and lots for carnivores too. Great value. ⓐ Kompagnistræde 20 ❶ 33150575 ⓦ www.rizraz.dk ⏱ 11.30–00.00 ⓝ Bus 6A; CityCirkel: Nationalmuseet or Stormbroen

AFTER DARK

RESTAURANTS

Apropos ££ ❸ During the day a smart café bar serving lunches to city workers, at night this place has a classier menu, an excellent wine list and modern fusion dishes. Vegetarian menu also. ⓐ Halmtorvet 12 ❶ 33231221 ⓦ www.cafeapropos.dk ⏱ 10.00–00.00 Sun–Thur, 10.00–01.00 Fri & Sat ⓝ Bus: 2A, 5A, 66, 250S; CityCirkel/S-train: København H

Bøf & Ost ££ ❹ Beautiful 18th-century building, and the best reputation in Copenhagen for a good *bøf* (steak). Also serves great fish and a wide selection of *ost* (cheese). ⓐ Gråbrødretorv 13 ❶ 33119911 ⓦ www.boef-ost.dk ⏱ 11.30–01.00 (kitchen closes 22.30) ⓝ Bus: 5A, 6A, 14; CityCirkel: Krystalgade or Fiolstræde; S-train: Nørreport

Sorte Hest ££ ❺ Sorte Hest has been at this location since 1903 and is currently run by a Michelin-starred Danish chef. Service and furnishing is inspired by the laid-back Latino eating culture, but there's nothing casual about the superb dishes served up to diners. ⓐ Vesterbrogade 135 ⓣ 33252223 ⓦ www.sortehestetspisested.dk ⓛ 12.00–15.00, 17.30–00.00 (kitchen closes 22.00) Wed–Fri ⓝ Bus: 6A

BARS & CLUBS

Cirkusbygninen (The Circus Building) Hosts the Wallmans Dinnershow. Multi-level seating, several bars and a good view of the performance. There is an after-show nightclub from 23.00 on performance days ⓐ Jernbanegade 8, off H C Andersens Boulevard ⓣ 33163700 ⓦ www.wallmans.dk ⓛ Event & opening hours vary: check website for details ⓝ Bus: 5A, 6A, 66; CityCirkel: Vesterport; S-train: Vesterport or København H

Copenhagen Jazz House The leading jazz club in the city. Live music three nights a week and Nat Clubben, the nightclub, at weekends. ⓐ Niels Hemmingssengade 10 ⓣ 33152600 ⓦ www.jazzhouse.dk ⓛ 18.00–00.00 Sun–Thur, 18.00–05.00 Fri & Sat ⓝ Bus: 5A, 6A, 14; CityCirkel: Gammeltorv; S-train: Nørreport. Admission charge

Mojo Live blues nightly. ⓐ Løngangstræde, near Rådhuspladsen ⓣ 33116453 ⓦ www.mojo.dk ⓛ 20.00–05.00. Admission charge ⓝ Bus 6A; CityCirkel: Nationalmuseet or Stormbroen

Pumphuset Live music every weekend by prominent artists in an intimate venue. ⓐ Studiestræde 52, near Axeltorv ⓣ 33931960 ⓝ Bus: 5A, 6A; CityCirkel: Axeltorv; S-train: Vesterport

Christianshavn & Slotsholmen

The two neighbouring islands of Slotsholmen and Christianshavn couldn't be more different. Slotsholmen is the political and financial heartland of the country. The Parliament meets here, and it was the home of the Royal Family until the palace burned down. Every inch of this tiny island, where the city of Copenhagen had its origins, is covered with landmark buildings.

Christianshavn, and Christiania especially, is a very different kettle of fish. Christiania exists on the fringes of the city's laws. Until recently its citizens, a motley combination of alternative types and sensible law-abiding people, paid no rates or rents and you could buy cannabis from stalls along so-called Pusher Street. Negotiations with the city's authorities over issues such as tax, drug laws and private vs collective ownership of land and property are ongoing. The rest of the island, Christianshavn, is a bijou area with many exclusive restaurants housed in renovated warehouses along the canal side.

SIGHTS & ATTRACTIONS

Bibliotekshaven (Royal Library Gardens)

This tranquil little garden is hidden down an alley off Rigsdagsgården. Almost perfect in design, it has a central pond, fountain and some very complacent ducks, pretty lawns and beautiful flower borders. Even Kierkegaard, usually a solemn figure, looks pleased to be here. ⓐ Rigsdagsgården ⓒ 06.00–22.00 ⓝ Harbour bus: Det Kongelige Bibliotek

Børsen (Stock Exchange)

Europe's oldest stock exchange, built between 1619 and 1640 by

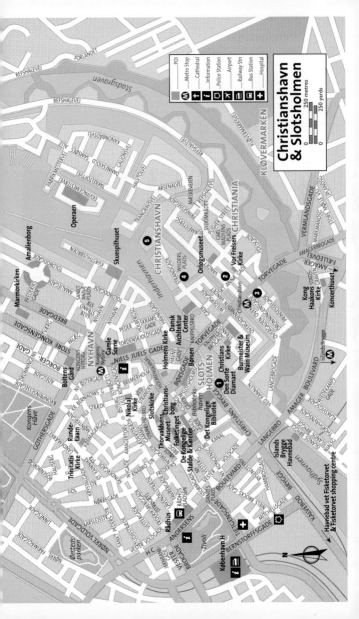

△ *Børsen, the old stock exchange*

Christian IV, who had grand plans for Copenhagen as the financial capital of Europe. Now the Chamber of Commerce, it is not open to the public, but you can stand outside and marvel at the fantasy architecture – a 54 m (177 ft) copper spire in the form of intertwining dragons' tails bearing three golden crowns at their ends, representing the three golden nations of Denmark, Sweden and Norway. The stonework is a riot of embellishments and excesses. ⓐ Børsgade
ⓝ Bus: 1A, 2A; CityCirkel: Christiansborg

Christiania
Just across the canal from Slotsholmen but far, far away culturally and economically, is Christiania. It is full of Peter Pans who flew

away in the 1970s and never went home, artists, alcoholics, and now tourists after the thrill of wandering around a genuinely alternative society. To see some quirky designer houses, go for a stroll around the lakes at the back.

Pusher Street, previously a drug haven, has been cleaned up, and quartets of Danish policemen wander around the place making sure that the stalls laden with hash don't reappear. The cafés, graffiti and wild pot plants still remain.

There are some excellent craft, clothes and antique shops, several good restaurants and live music venues, stalls selling bongs and pipes, ethnic clothes, and right at the entrance a good café and information centre. The most popular souvenir is the Free Christiania t-shirt. Note that there are no ATM machines in Christiania and no-one accepts credit cards. You should also refrain from taking photographs. ⓐ Prinsessgade ☏ 32956507 Ⓦ www.christiania.org ⓛ Information centre: 12.00–18.00 Mon–Thur, 12.00–16.00 Fri; guided tours: 15.00 July & Aug ⓝ Bus: 66; harbour bus: Knippelsbro; metro: Christianshavn

Christiansborg Slot (Christiansborg Palace)

Vast labyrinth of buildings, a maze if you don't know what to look for. The Danish tendency to make signs unobtrusive has been taken to a fine art here and it is possible to wander right through the place without noticing any of the doors you need to call in at.

A castle of some sort has stood here since 1147 although the present edifice dates back only to the early 20th century. The best approach to the palace is over the Marble Bridge across Frederiksholm Canal and into the outer courtyard of the palace. Over to your left across a parade ground an unadorned and bolted door is the entrance to the Royal Reception Rooms, the only bit of the Royal Family's part of the palace that you can visit.

Grandiose halls are lined with elaborate inlaid marble, and there is beautiful hand-painted wood panelling and a series of brilliantly coloured tapestries by Bjørn Nørgaard telling the story of Denmark. Also in here is the fascinating portrait of the Royal Family which includes several heads of European states and which you will see reproduced in several of the other royal palaces. The palace houses the Parliament, the Supreme Court and the Prime Minister's office. ⓐ Slotsholmen ❶ 33926494 Ⓦ www.ses.dk ⏰ 10.00–16.00 (closed Mon, Oct–Apr); tours in English: 15.00 May–Sept Ⓝ Bus: 1A, 2A, 15, 26, 29; CityCirkel: Christiansborg. Admission charge

Christiansborg Slotskirke (Palace Chapel)

Copenhagen has a history of fires and this church, built in 1826, is

no exception. After surviving a major fire in 1884 that destroyed the palace, this church was nearly devastated during restoration work in the early 1990s, when a firework set the scaffolding alight and destroyed the roof. Designed by the architect C F Hansen, its neoclassical marble interior, beautiful ceiling friezes by Thorvaldsen and reliefs by Karen Blixen are a treat. It is a quiet place to retreat from the traffic whirling around Slotsplads. Services are no longer held here.

ⓐ Christiansborg Slotsplads, near Thorvaldsens Museet on Vindebrogade ❶ 33926451 ⓦ www.ses.dk ❶ 12.00–16.00 Sun, Easter, July & autumn school holidays (check website for exact dates) ⓝ Bus: 1A, 2A, 15, 26, 29; CityCirkel: Christiansborg

⬤ Christiania is a great place for connoisseurs of outdoor art

Folketinget (Danish Parliament)

Out from the arch between the two wings of the palace brings
you into Christiansborg Slotsplads, the main square in front of the
Parliament building where most political protests are held. Round
the side is the unmarked entrance to the Parliament. You can
wander up to the public gallery while the 179 Parliament members
are sitting or take the tour in English. This lets you see the enormous
Vandrehal (Hall of Wanderers), where the Danish Constitution
is kept. ❸ Rigsdagsgården ❶ 33375500 ❾ www.folketinget.dk
🕒 During parliamentary session (call for times); tours: 14.00 Sun
🚌 Bus: 1A, 2A, 15, 26, 29; CityCirkel: Christiansborg

Gammel Strand

Across the bridge by the Slotskirke is a laid-back, canal-side street,
great for a coffee and Danish while you rest from sightseeing.
The street has an ancient history: in medieval times fishermen
landed their catch here and fresh fish was sold along this road
by fishwives, one of whom is commemorated in the statue by the
bridge. Lots of the cafés here still base their cuisine on fish. At no. 48
is Kunstforegningen, an exhibition space for good photography.
🚌 Bus 6A; CityCirkel: Nationalmuseet or Stormbroen

Holmens Kirke (Navy Church)

The Church of the Royal Navy stands just across the canal from
Børsen and was originally built in 1562 as a naval forge. Around the
time that construction of Børsen began the building was converted
into a church for the navy and the present structure came into
being in 1649. The austere Lutheran exterior gives way inside to
a highly ornate pulpit and carved oak altarpiece. Several important
figures from Danish naval history are interred in the burial chapel

and the present Queen took her marriage vows here. ⓐ Holmens Kanal 9 ❶ 33136178 Ⓦ www.holmenskirke.dk 🕐 09.00–14.00 Mon–Fri, 09.00–12.00 Sat, for services only Sun Ⓝ Bus: 1A, 2A, 15, 26, 29; CityCirkel: Vingårdsstræde

De Kongelige Stalde & Kareter (Royal Stables & Coaches)

The outer courtyard of the palace is still used as a working training ground and exercise yard for the royal horses, used on state occasions for the royal carriages. The stables themselves survived the fire in 1794 and once housed 200 animals. In those days even royal horses lived lavish lifestyles, as can be seen from the marble columns and vaulted ceilings. The royal carriages and an ancient Bentley also have a home here. ⓐ Christiansborg Ridebane ❶ 33926300 Ⓦ www.ses.dk 🕐 14.00–16.00 Sat & Sun, Oct–Apr; 14.00–16.00 Fri–Sun, May–Sept Ⓝ Bus: 1A, 2A, 15, 26, 29; CityCirkel: Christiansborg

Ruinerne Under Christiansborg (Christiansborg Ruins)

Hidden away inside the arch which joins the royal and governmental sections of Christiansborg Palace are the excavated foundations of several earlier buildings, including those of the city's original fortress (see page 14).

In a clearly different style are the remains of the *Blå Tårn* (Blue Tower), Denmark's one-time major prison. Princess Eleonore Christine, daughter of Christian IV, was held here for allegedly being involved in a plot against her father. The ruins are laid out in the centre of a circular walkway with spotlights highlighting identifiable parts of the older buildings. Rooms off the central area display artefacts discovered during the excavations. Captions are in English and work well to clarify what you are actually looking at, and the dim light and sounds of dripping water add an air of mystery. ⓐ Christiansborg Slot ❶ 33926492

DEN SORTE DIAMANT (THE BLACK DIAMOND)

In contrast to the rest of the 17th-century Det Kongelige Bibliotek (The Royal Library), with its red brick and Boston ivy homeliness, is the startling modernity of its black granite and glass extension. Up close there is a definite sense of vertigo as the building sheers off towards the water's edge, reflections of the surrounding buildings on the smooth black surface adding to the sense of confusion. Inside, across sandstone floors, the escalator brings you to a huge library of books and a walkway to the old library. In the basement is the National Photography Museum, which has a changing series of exhibits. Outside the building, students lounge about in café deckchairs, drinking coffee and soaking up the sun. There is also a fine dining restaurant called **Søren K** (🕐 12.00–00.00 Mon–Sat), a less formal café Øjeblikket (see page 102) and a good bookshop.

🅰 Søren Kierkegaard Plads, by Det Kongelige Bibliotek
🛈 33474747 🅦 www.kb.dk 🕐 Library open 10.00–19.00 Mon–Fri, 10.00–14.00 Sat 🅝 Harbour bus: Det Kongelige Bibliotek

🅦 www.ses.dk 🕐 10.00–16.00 May–Sept; 10.00–16.00 Tues–Sun, Oct–Apr
🅝 Bus: 1A, 2A, 15, 26, 29; CityCirkel: Christiansborg. Admission charge

Vor Frelsers Kirke (Our Saviour's Church)

En route to Christiania along Sankt Annæ Gade you'll pass this 1696 church with its baroque altar and a huge organ resting on the backs of two stucco elephants. The real reason to visit is the trip up the 400 steps to the top of the spire, the last 150 of them being on the outside of the building. Not a journey for those of a nervous disposition, but if you can brace yourself against the vertigo there are some stunning views from the top. King Christian was the first to make the climb, in 1752 when the tower was inaugurated. If you are here when there is a church service it is worth hanging about to hear the organ being played. ⓐ Sankt Annæ Gade 29 ① 32546883 ⓦ www.vorfrelserskirke.dk ① 11.00–16.30 Mon–Sat, 12.00–16.00 Sun Apr–Aug; 11.00–15.30 Mon–Sat, 12.00–15.30 Sun, Sept–Mar, Tower closed Nov–Mar ⓝ Bus: 66; CityCirkel: Gammeltorv; metro: Christianshavn. Admission charge for the tower

CULTURE

Dansk Arkitektur Center (Danish Architecture Centre)

Housed in a 19th-century warehouse on the harbour (itself a beautiful stone and wood building), the centre is involved in most of the design and architectural projects in Copenhagen and internationally. On the ground floor is a bookshop (see page 101) and an exhibition which changes regularly; on the second floor is a great café with harbour views. ⓐ Strandgade 27B ① 32571930 ⓦ www.dac.dk ① 10.00–17.00 Thur–Tues, 10.00–21.00 Wed ⓝ Bus: 2A, 66, 350S; harbour bus: Knippelsbro; metro: Christianshavn. Admission charge for exhibition (free from 17.00 Wed)

Operaen (Opera House)

Donated by the A P Møller and Chastine McKinney Møller foundation (founders of the shipping company Mærsk), the Opera House is entirely the work of Danish artists and designers. The imposing exterior, designed by architect Henning Larsen, is controversial but impressive. Located in Holmen, across the harbour from Amalienborg, nothing is cheap in this building. You can take guided tours (recommended), eat in the restaurant or watch a performance, but be prepared to part with at least 100kr. ⓐ Ekvipagemestervej 10 ☎ 33696933 ⓦ www.operaen.dk ⏰ Tours: 09.30, 16.30 Sat & Sun ⓝ Bus: 66; harbour bus: Operaen ❶ Book tours in advance

Orlogsmuseet (Royal Danish Naval Museum)

Set in a former naval hospital in Christianshavn, the museum houses over 300 model boats built from the 16th to the 19th century. Many were working models made by the men who built the real thing, to show to their sponsors, and range from cutaway models to fully rigged, seagoing but tiny ships. There are also carved wooden figureheads, beautiful brass instruments and a replica submarine, plus a café. ⓐ Overgaden Oven Vandet 58 ☎ 33116037 ⓦ www.orlogsmuseet.dk ⏰ 12.00–16.00 Tues–Sun ⓝ Bus: 2A, 66; harbour bus: Knippelsbro; metro: Christianshavn. Admission charge

Thorvaldsens Museet

Museum focusing on the sculptures of Bertel Thorvaldsen (1768–1844), one of Denmark's most famous sons. As a sculptor he made his name in Rome while learning his craft and was heavily influenced by Greek and Roman statuary. His return to Copenhagen towards the end of his life brought about an artistic revival in the city. His output bordered on the manic and this museum, purpose-built at the expense of the Royal Family, houses masses of his work. The ground floor consists largely of monumentally huge plaster casts which were used in the creation of his great works of statuary, set along long corridors beautifully lit by natural light. The upper storey of the building contains his personal art collection. In the corridors you will meet Byron, Walter Scott, Christ and figures from Greek and Roman mythology. Be sure to look up at the ceilings in each room, as they

are all unique. 🅐 Bertel Thorvaldsens Plads 2, off Vindebrogade
🅣 33321532 🅦 www.thorvaldsensmuseum.dk 🅛 10.00–17.00 Tues–Sun
🅝 Bus: 1A, 2A, 15, 26, 29; CityCirkel: Nationalmuseet, Stormbroen or
Christiansborg. Admission charge (free Wed & for under 18s)

RETAIL THERAPY

Stroll across the bridge from Christiansborg and browse the shops on
the right hand side of Knippelsbrogade. When you reach the canal,
cross over and explore the small jewellery, clothing and home furnishing
shops in the side streets between Knippelsbrogade and Christiania.

Carl Madsens Plads Open-air market in Christiania where you can
buy politically oriented t-shirts, ethnic woollens, skunk seed, bongs
and the like. 🅛 11.00–late (times vary) 🅝 Bus: 2A, 66, 350S; harbour
bus: Knippelsbro; metro: Christianshavn

Christiania Bikes Fun to browse, even if you won't fit one of their bikes
on the plane. 🅐 Refshalevej 2 🅣 32548748 🅦 www.christianiabikes.dk
🅛 09.00–17.00 Mon–Fri, 10.00–14.00 Sat 🅝 Bus: 2A, 66, 350S;
harbour bus: Knippelsbro; metro: Christianshavn

Dansk Arkitektur Center Book Shop Housed in the old dock area,
the Nordic region's largest collection of Danish and international
design and architecture books. 🅐 Strandgade 27B 🅣 32571930
🅦 www.dac.dk 🅛 10.00–17.00 Mon–Fri 🅝 Bus: 2A, 66, 350S;
harbour bus: Knippelsbro; metro: Christianshavn

Gammel Strand Flea Market Flea market open from spring to
autumn, with good antiques. 🅛 09.00–18.00 Fri, 09.00–15.00 Sat

Bus: 1A, 2A, 6A; CityCirkel: Nationalmuseet or Stormbroen; metro: Christianshavn

Kvindesmedien The women's blacksmith shop makes all sorts of handicrafts out of metal. Mælkevejen 83E 32577658 www.kvindesmedien.dk 09.00–17.00 Mon–Fri, 11.00–15.00 Sat Bus: 2A, 66, 350S; harbour bus: Knippelsbro; metro: Christianshavn

TAKING A BREAK

Head out past Vor Frelsers Kirke toward the canals and you'll find canal-side bars and cafés along Sankt Annæ Gade. In Slotsholmen the place to relax is Øieblikket, in the lobby of the new library, or pop over to Gammel Strand, great for coffee, beer, lunch or just people-watching.

Øjeblikket £ Good cakes and sandwiches; deckchairs in summer looking out over the waterfront. Søren Kierkegaards Plads 1, inside Den Sorte Diamant 09.00–19.00 Mon–Sat Harbour bus: Det Kongelige Bibliotek

Oven Vande Café ££ A popular café by day and restaurant by night, with year-round outdoor seating. Serves a great brunch. Overgaden Oven Vandet 44 32959602 www.cafeovenvande.dk 10.00–00.00 (kitchen closes 22.00) Bus: 2A, 66; harbour bus: Knippelsbro; metro: Christianshavn

AFTER DARK

RESTAURANTS
Bottega ££ Casual, modern, southern Italian-style food and an

extensive wine list. Also offers great take-away. ⓐ Dronningensgade 42
ⓣ Restaurant: 32955571; take-away: 32955565 Ⓦ www.bottega.nu
Ⓛ 12.00–00.00 Ⓝ Bus: 66, 2A, 350S; harbour bus: Knippelsbro;
metro: Christianshavn

Restaurant Kanalen £££ ❹ High-class restaurant on the canal.
Busy and traditionally Danish at lunch, but candle-lit, romantic
and French-inspired cuisine at night. ⓐ Wilders Plads 2 ⓣ 32951338
Ⓦ www.restaurant-kanalen.dk Ⓛ 11.30–00.00 Mon–Sat (kitchen:
11.30–15.00, 17.30–22.00) Ⓝ Bus: 2A, 66, 350S; harbour bus: Knippelsbro;
metro: Christianshavn

Noma £££+ ❺ Style, substance and two Michelin stars are the
draws at this converted 18th-century warehouse, where local
ingredients and methods of cooking have been used to make a very
original menu. ⓐ Strandgade 93 ⓣ 32963297 Ⓦ www.noma.dk
Ⓛ 18.00–01.00 Mon–Sat (kitchen closes 22.00) Ⓝ Bus: 2A, 66, 350S;
harbour bus: Knippelsbro; metro: Christianshavn

BARS & CLUBS
Loppen Laid-back club and performance venue in the heart of
Christiania. Big names as well as smaller bands. ⓐ Christiania
Sydområdet 4b ⓣ 32578422 Ⓦ www.loppen.dk Ⓛ 21.00–late Wed–Sat
Ⓝ Bus: 2A, 66, 350S; harbour bus: Knippelsbro; metro: Christianshavn

Ruby Popular bar and club with great cocktails, a snazzy interior
design and lovely outdoor seating. ⓐ Nybrogade 10, Gammel Strand
ⓣ 33931203 Ⓦ www.rby.dk Ⓛ 16.00–01.00 Mon–Wed, 16.00–02.00
Thur–Sat Ⓝ Bus: 6A; CityCirkel: Nationalmuseet or Stormbroen
ⓘ Minimum age 25

Around the Three Lakes

Three man-made lakes, Sortedams Sø, Peblinge Sø and Sankt Jørgens Sø, mark the northwestern boundary of the city centre. To the west of these lie the suburbs of Nørrebro, Copenhagen's bohemian quarter, and Østerbro, with its stadium and park. To the east are the Botanical Gardens, Rosenberg Slot and Statens Museum for Kunst (the Danish National Gallery). Around the lakes themselves are some of Copenhagen's most exclusive apartment blocks, and a network of paths. On summer afternoons they come alive with Copenhageners jogging, strolling and meeting up with friends and family.

SIGHTS & ATTRACTIONS

Blågårdsgade

Slightly more bohemian than Sankt Hans Torv is this pedestrianised street off Nørrebrogade, full of interesting cafés and with a multicultural feel. Immigrant communities have settled in the area, establishing inexpensive ethnic restaurants and grocery stores. Blågårds Plads, with its many restaurants and cafés, turns into an ice skating rink in winter. ❷ Bus: 5A, 350S

Botanisk Have & Museum (Botanical Gardens & Museum)

Built in 1874, the 10 hectare (25 acre) Botanical Gardens were originally part of the city's defensive ramparts. The moat and walls are now a garden pond and rockery. The garden is filled year round with excellent planting, which offers pretty bowers, shaded walks, a well laid-out tropical and subtropical glasshouse and an orchid house. Also within the grounds is the small Botanical Museum, part of the Natural History Museum. ❸ Øster Farimagsgade 2B ❶ 35322222

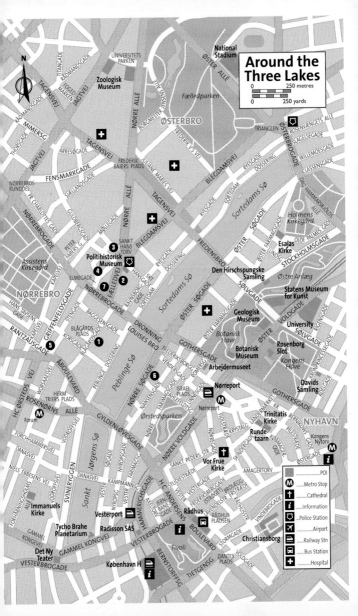

ⓦ www.botanik.snm.ku.dk ⓛ Gardens: 08.30–18.00 May–Sept;
08.30–16.00 Tues–Sun, Oct–Apr (museum hours vary) ⓝ Bus: 5A,
6A, 14, 350S; CityCirkel/metro/S-train: Nørreport

Fælledparken

To the northeast of trendy Nørrebro is this expansive green area.
It has a classy skateboarding park, an open-air pool, children's
play areas, imaginative planting and a good café. It is also home
to the huge **National Stadium** (ⓐ Parken, Øster Allé 50 ⓣ 35437400
ⓦ www.fck.dk). There are often free concerts here and many
impromptu football games. A good place for a break from the
city centre, where you can join ordinary Danes in enjoying some
leisure time. ⓝ Bus: 1A, 3A, 42, 184, 185, 150S

Kongens Have (The King's Gardens)

Copenhagen's oldest park, created as the private gardens of
Christian IV when he built Rosenborg Slot and laid out in a series
of grids that can still be observed today. It's full of huge old trees,
with a pretty hedged garden and a pond full of very self-satisfied
ducks. A popular spot for sunbathing and picnicking, and a good
café. Kids will love the playground and puppet theatre in summer.
ⓐ Gothersgade ⓦ www.ses.dk ⓛ 07.00–17.00 Jan; 07.00–18.00
Feb–14 Mar & 15 Oct–Dec; 07.00–19.00 1–14 Oct; 07.00–20.00 15–31
Mar; 07.00–21.00 Apr & Sept; 07.00–22.00 May–Aug ⓛ Bus: 350S;
CityCirkel: Kongens Have; metro/S-train: Nørreport

Nansensgade

This is one of Copenhagen's delightful quarters that often goes
undiscovered by tourists. The village-like atmosphere on this street
is not to be missed – you can easily spend a few hours here wandering

▲ Fountain in Kongens Have, with Cupid on a swan

around the small clothes shops and home-furnishing boutiques. There are plenty of cafés – check out the freaky and popular Bankerot, meaning 'bankrupt'. Some of the city's best pizzerias and ice cream parlours are here too. Bus: 2A, 5A; CityCirkel/metro/S-train: Nørreport

Rosenborg Slot (Rosenborg Castle)

Lovely, popular little castle built by Christian IV , telling the history of the Danish kings from the 16th to the 19th century. The place was built in the 17th century by Christian IV as a summer palace and from the 18th century, when one of the King Frederiks built a bigger home at Frederiksborg, it was used to store the royal heirlooms. You can see the royal tableware, including glass knives and forks, a solid silver table, huge silver lions and heaps of portraits, all chronologically arranged as you walk around the rooms. The dazzling crown jewels are in the basement. Busy at peak times. Øster Voldgade 4A 33153286 www.rosenborgslot.dk 11.00–14.00 Tues–Sun, Jan–Apr, Nov & Dec (11.00–16.00 in spring & Easter school holidays); 10.00–16.00 May, Sept & Oct; 10.00–17.00 June–Aug Bus: 5A, 6A, 350S; CityCirkel/metro/S-train: Nørreport. Admission charge

Rundetaarn (The Round Tower)

Another of Christian IV's creations, Rundetaarn was completed in 1642. The tower is part of the 'Trinitatis complex' and linked to an observatory, a student church and a university library. It has a unique 209 m (686 ft) spiral ramp and a short narrow stairwell to the very top. As well as being the oldest functioning observatory in Europe, the tower often holds interesting art and photo exhibitions, seminars and conferences, and classical music concerts. Fantastic views over the rooftops of Copenhagen. Købmagergade 52A 33730373 www.rundetaarn.dk 10.00–17.00 mid-Sept–mid-May; 10.00–20.00

Architecture straight out of Hans Christian Andersen – Rosenborg Slot

mid-May–mid-Sept; observatory: 19.00–22.00 Tues & Wed, mid-Oct–mid-Mar; 13.00–16.00 Sun, July–mid-Aug ⊘ Bus: 6A, 5A; CityCirkel: Rundtaarn; metro/S-train: Nørreport

Sankt Hans Torv

The centre of cool Nørrebro, Sankt Hans Torv is a small square which forms the junction of several intersecting streets. Fælledvej, Elmegade and Guldbergsgade are home to some of the city's best eateries, bars and night haunts and quirky, local fashion boutiques. This area is where all the really tuned-in Copenhageners hang out, including assorted younger Royals. In summer afternoons the pavement tables fill with the chattering classes and the evenings are enlivened with clubbers. ⊘ Bus: 3A, 5A, 350S

CULTURE

Arbejdermuseet (The Workers' Museum)

No Danish design items in this engaging little museum dedicated to the working lives of Copenhagen's citizens. Progressing through the various incarnations of Danish home life, this encapsulates the hardship of many of the city's working people in a series of recreated rooms. Text is only in Danish but the images are graphic enough to tell the story well. Overcrowding and poverty give way gradually to comfort with the few essential items of the 19th century (an overturned table for a bed, primitive contraceptives, cheap, ineffective medicines) replaced by gramophones, washing machines, table lamps and three-piece suites. Recreated in its entirety is the apartment of the Sørenson family, unaltered from 1915 to 1990, when the daughter finally gave everything to the museum. The café is another old-school Copenhagen construct, selling traditional food

🔺 *The Hirschsprung Collection has an intimate, domestic setting*

and drinks. 🅰 Rømersgade 22 📞 33932575 🌐 www.arbejdermuseet.dk
🕐 10.00–16.00 🚍 Bus: 5A, 350S; CityCirkel/metro/S-train: Nørreport.
Admission charge

Den Hirschsprungske Samling (The Hirschsprung Collection)

Denmark's finest collection of 19th- and early 20th-century Danish art
was tobacco manufacturer Heinrich Hirschsprung's gift to the Danish
State, with the pre-condition that it be housed in an intimate setting.
The neoclassical building contains a series of small rooms where
exhibits are displayed, designed to reproduce their original setting in
the German–Jewish immigrant's own home. The collection includes
works by Danish artist C W Eckberg and his students Christian Købke
and William Bende. The gallery is often forgotten by visitors in the
art overload of its neighbour, the Statens Museum for Kunst. Check

STATENS MUSEUM FOR KUNST (NATIONAL GALLERY)
This was originally the private art collection of the Danish
Royals, who decided to let the nation share their treasures.
The permanent collection covers seven centuries of painting.
A stunning modern extension at the back, designed by Danish
architect Anna Maria Indrio, now houses temporary exhibitions
of statuary. The huge glass north wall of the museum forms a
panoramic rural scene in summer. There is a children's section,
regular concerts and performances in the foyer, changing
exhibitions and a good café and bookshop. ③ Sølvgade 48
🕿 33748494 🌐 www.smk.dk 🕒 10.00–17.00 Tues & Thur–Sun,
10.00–20.00 Wed 🚌 Bus: 6A, 14, 26, 40, 42, 43, 184, 185, 150S;
metro/S-train: Nørreport or Østerport, then ten-minute walk

out the tobacco theme in the lobby with the mosaic floor and the
portrait of the city's benefactor. ③ Stockholmsgade 20 🕿 35420336
🌐 www.hirschsprung.dk 🕒 11.00–16.00 Wed–Mon 🚌 Bus: 6A, 150S,
14, 40, 184, 185; CityCirkel/metro/S-train: Nørreport

Zoologisk Museum (Zoological Museum)
Not to be confused with the actual zoo beside Frederiksberg
Slot (see page 83), this museum is part of the Natural History
Museum and is for stuffed creatures only. One section is dedicated
to animals that have adapted to urban living, while others contain
massive walruses, a 14 m (46 ft) long skeleton of a bowhead whale,
polar bears and lots of insects. There is also a children's section.
③ Universitetsparken 15 🕿 35322222 🌐 www.zoologi.snm.ku.dk
🕒 10.00–17.00 Tues–Sun 🚌 Bus: 18, 150S. Admission charge

RETAIL THERAPY

There is much to see and buy in the area around the Three Lakes,
chiefly to the northeast in hip Nørrebro. Blågårdsgade and Elmegade
have a bohemian atmosphere and are full of alternative shops. There
is a Saturday flea market along the yellow wall of the Assistens
Kirkegård and another at Israel Plads close to Nørreport station.
Frederiksborggade has designer clothes and home accessory shops.
Ravnsborggade is literally lined with antique shops – Montan Antik
Design at no. 17 and Veirhanen at no. 12 are worth searching out.

TAKING A BREAK

Floras Kaffebar £ ❶ Popular spot to brunch or lunch. Order
anything on the menu to take away. ⓐ Blågårdsgade 27 ❶ 35390018
🅦 www.floraskaffebar.dk 🕓 10.00–22.00 Mon–Thur, 10.00–23.00 Fri
& Sat, 10.00–20.00 Sun (kitchen closes 1 hr earlier) ⓝ Bus: 5A

Picnic £ ❷ Organic *meze*-style lunch. Eat in or take away.
ⓐ Fælledvej 22B ❶ 35390953 🕓 11.00–22.00 ⓝ Bus: 5A, 350S

Sebastopol £–££ ❸ Trendy French-style café, excellent breakfasts
and lunches. Order at the bar. ⓐ Sankt Hans Torv 2 ❶ 35363002
🅦 www.sebastopol.dk 🕓 08.00–00.00 Mon–Wed, 08.00–02.00
Thur & Fri, 09.00–02.00 Sat, 09.00–00.00 Sun ⓝ Bus: 5A, 350S

The Laundromat Café ££ ❹ Trendy retro café, and yes,
it really is a laundry. Loungy music. ⓐ Elmegade 15 ❶ 35352672
🕓 08.00–00.00 Mon–Thur, 10.00–02.00 Fri & Sat ⓝ Bus: 5A, 350S

AFTER DARK

RESTAURANTS

Scarpetta £ ❺ Voted the city's best new restaurant in 2009, this lovely bright Italian eatery serves top-notch food at bottom-notch (by Copenhagen standards) prices. ⓐ Ranztausgade 7 ❶ 35350808 ⓦ www.cofoco.dk ⓒ 17.30–23.30 (kitchen closes 21.30) ⓝ Bus: 66, 69

Bibendum ££ ❻ Serving only tapas, cheese and charcuterie, Bibendum is famed for its fantastic wine collection with over 50 varieties served by the glass. Reservations recommended in evening. ⓐ Nansensgade 45 ❶ 33330774 ⓦ www.vincafe.dk ⓒ 16.00–00.00 Mon–Sat ⓝ Bus: 5A, 6A, 14, 350S; metro/S-train: Nørreport

Gefährlich ££ ❼ A two-storey restaurant, cocktail bar and nightclub which also houses a hairdresser, clothing shop and art gallery. Good menu and excellent DJs playing funk, soul and disco classics. ⓐ Fælledvej 7 ❶ 35241324 ⓦ www.gefahrlich.dk ⓒ 17.00–01.00 Tues, 17.00–03.00 Wed & Thur, 17.00–04.30 Fri & Sat (kitchen closes 23.00) ⓝ Bus: 5A, 350S

CLUB

Rust One of the liveliest clubs and live music venues in town, with two floors and three small bars. Over 21s only. ⓐ Guldbergsgade 8 ❶ 35245200 ⓦ www.rust.dk ⓒ 21.00–05.00 Wed–Sat ⓝ Bus: 5A, 350S. Admission charge for nightclub and some concerts

❿ *Zealand's beaches are only a short trip from the capital*

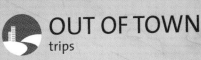

OUT OF TOWN
trips

The Øresund Coast

Copenhagen lies on the eastern side of the island of Zealand, or 'Sjælland'. Along its northeastern shore, served by an efficient Kystbanen regional rail service as well as partly by the S-train, lies the Danish Riviera which faces out onto Øresund. To take in all of the sights you need a few days, but you can mix and match if time is short.

Elsinor, or 'Helsingør' is the furthest point on this trip at 47 km (29 miles) from Copenhagen, about 45 minutes by train. Before that, you'll find the Louisiana Museum of Modern Art in Humlebæk (32 minutes by train), Bakken Amusement Park (20 minutes) and Charlottenlund (15 minutes) with its beaches and the Akvarium. The Experimentarium is just outside Copenhagen in Hellerup. The open-air Frilandsmuseet in Lyngby (see page 148) is great for children.

SIGHTS & ATTRACTIONS

Charlottenlund Beach & Danmarks Akvarium

The Danish Riviera begins at Charlottenlund Beach, a popular, scenic green area with a tiny strip of sand and nice views over Copenhagen harbour. To one side is a private bathing area with its own café, toilets and showers and separate nude bathing places for men and women. There is also a picnic area. Close by are the remains of Charlottenlund Fort, now a campsite.

Most visitors come for the Akvarium, with over 300 species of fish and water creatures, including piranhas, crocodiles, sharks and a coelacanth preserved in alcohol. You can watch the animals being fed and at weekends there are touch pools. ❸ Kavalergården 1 ❶ 39623283 ❿ www.akvarium.dk ❶ 10.00–16.00 Nov–Jan;

BAKKEN AMUSEMENT PARK & BELLEVUE BEACH

Founded in 1583, Bakken Amusement Park lays claim to being the oldest in the world. Popular with Copenhagen families since the 35 rides are bigger and cheaper than Tivoli and admission to the park itself is free. There are beer halls, gaming arcades, a shooting gallery, and at night a popular revue show, together with lots of cafés and restaurants.

Next door is Jægersborg Dyrehaven, a vast expanse of parkland with free roaming deer. Close by is Bellevue beach, a popular sunbathing spot with open green spaces, good eating and clear water. Look out for the Arne Jacobsen influence in the area, particularly the petrol station. ⓐ Dyrehavsbakken, Dyrehavej 62, Klampenborg ⓣ 39962096 ⓦ www.bakken.dk ⓛ Mar–Aug, times vary so check website ⓜ S-train/Kystbanen: Klampenborg. Admission charge for rides

10.00–17.00 Feb–May, Sept & Oct; 10.00–18.00 June–Aug; open until 20.00 Wed, Feb–Aug ⓜ S-train: Charlottenlund. Admission charge

Experimentarium

Northeast of Østerbro in Hellerup lies the Experimentarium. This is a hands-on science centre housed in the former Tuborg bottling factory, and it is great for kids. The centre offers piloted tours explaining the various aspects of science which affect our lives. All the exhibits are designed to get people involved, from gyroscopes to making cheese to wandering through a hall of mirrors. The exhibits change regularly but there are constant troops of children storming around. The afternoon is generally quieter. ⓐ Tuborg Havnevej 7 ⓣ 39273333

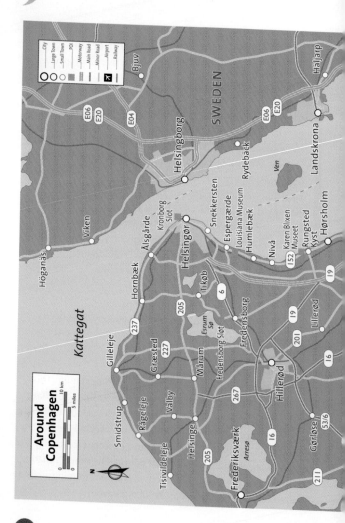

Around Copenhagen

Kattegat

SWEDEN

Helsingborg

Landskrona

Häljarp

Bjuv

Höganäs

Viken

Helsingør

Kronborg Slot

Snekkersten

Espergærde

Rydebäck

Ven

Louisiana Museum

Humlebæk

Nivå

Karen Blixen Museet

Rungsted Kyst

Hørsholm

Ålsgårde

Hornbæk

Tikøb

Gilleleje

Fredensborg

Esrum Sø

Mårum

Fredensborg Slot

Græsted

Rågeleje

Valby

Helsinge

Smidstrup

Tisvildeleje

Arresø

Frederiksværk

Hillerød

Lillerød

Gørløse

118

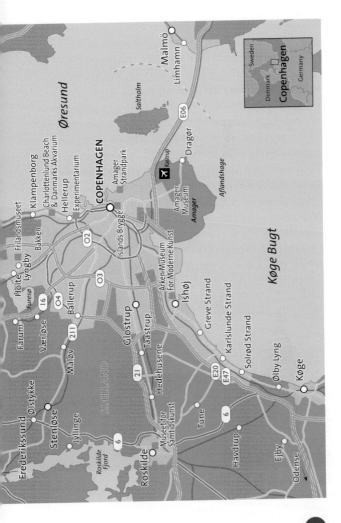

Ⓦ www.experimentarium.dk Ⓛ 09.30–17.00 Mon & Wed–Fri,
09.30–21.00 Tues, 11.00–17.00 Sat & Sun Ⓝ Bus: 1A, 14; S-train:
Hellerup then 15-minute walk. Admission charge

Helsingør & Kronborg Slot (Kronborg Castle)

Kronborg Castle, Shakespeare's setting for *Hamlet*, was originally
a large toll collection point for ships entering the narrow Øresund.
It became a castle in 1574, when Frederick II took a liking to the spot.
Burned down by accident in 1629, rebuilt and then ravaged by the
Swedes in 1658, it was again restored in 1922. You can now visit the
Danish Maritime Museum, the king's chambers, the chapel and
the dungeons. The chief draw is the king's quarters, a complete
fabrication but with genuine artefacts brought in from other
sites. The ship museum is interesting, as is the pretty, completely
reconstructed, chapel, but the dungeon is a real horror – don't go
there if you are at all claustrophobic. The real highlight is the

🔵 *Kronborg Castle – Elsinore without Hamlet*

building itself, set on a promontory of land and looking very much as though Hamlet could pop up on the battlements at any moment.

The rest of Helsingør contains, as well as lots of Swedes who flock here for the (relatively) cheaper alcohol, antique shops and an excellent town museum. Just northwest of town is Marienlyst Slot, an 18th-century manor house with exhibits of local paintings and silverware.

Helsingør Bymuseum Ⓐ Sankt Anna Gade 36 ❶ 49281800 Ⓦ www.visithelsingor.dk ❷ 10.00–16.00 Tues–Fri, 10.00–14.00 Sat, 12.00–16.00 Sun. Admission charge

Kronborg Slot Ⓐ Kronborg 2 ❶ 49213078 Ⓦ www.kronborgslot.dk ❷ 10.30–17.00 May–Sept; 11.00–15.00 Tues–Sun, Jan–Mar; 11.00–16.00 Tues–Sun, Apr & Oct–Dec. Admission charge

Marienlyst Slot Ⓐ Marienlyst Allé 32 ❶ 49281830 Ⓦ www.helsingor.dk ❷ 12.00–16.00. Admission charge

CULTURE

Karen Blixen Museet

A memorial and museum for one of Denmark's greatest writers, set up in the house in which she was born. You can see exhibitions relating to her house as well as her life, work, drawings and paintings. Tours in English available on prior arrangement. Ⓐ Rungsted Strandvej 111, Rungsted Kyst ❶ 45571057 Ⓦ www.karen-blixen.dk ❷ 10.00–17.00 Tues–Sun, May–Sept; 13.00–16.00 Wed–Fri, 11.00–16.00 Sat & Sun, Oct–Apr Ⓝ Kystbanen: Rungsted Kyst, then 20-minute walk or bus: 388. Admission charge

Louisiana Museum of Modern Art

Don't miss a visit to this superb modern art museum, founded in 1954 by a private collector, Knud Jensen, in a 19th-century villa on

the Øresund. Helped by funding from the Carlsberg Foundation, it is now a circular series of single-storey galleries around a garden of amazing statues. The huge glass walls of many of the galleries give the impression that galleries, garden and sea are all part of one strangely lit, complex whole. The weather and the sea play an enormous part in how you experience the exhibits.

The collection includes works by Lichtenstein, Warhol and Oldenburg, and also Picasso, Francis Bacon, Giacometti and Rothko. There is also art by a group of left-wing abstract artists formed in 1948 known as the CoBrA movement after the first letters of the

names of their home cities (Copenhagen, Brussels and Amsterdam). In the garden, Henry Moore's *Bronze Woman* and statues by Max Ernst, Alexander Calder, Joan Miró and Giacometti sit in their own corners. There is an indoor children's area where kids can take part in art workshops and a clever playground in the garden. You will also find an excellent café and shop. ⓐ Gl Strandvej 13, Humlebæk ⓘ 49190719 ⓦ www.louisiana.dk ⓛ 11.00–22.00 Tues–Fri, 11.00–18.00 Sat & Sun ⓝ Kystbanen or regional train to Humlebæk, then 15-minute walk or bus: 388. Admission charge, free for under 18s

◗ *Pop-art heaven at the Louisiana*

RETAIL THERAPY

The museum shop at Louisiana, aside from the usual postcards, books and ornaments, has great soft furnishings and clothes. Kronborg Castle has good souvenirs and Christmas decorations, glassware and hand-woven garments.

The three main pedestrianised shopping streets in Helsingør are Stengade, Stjernegade and Bjergegade. Along Bjergegade check out Baagø, an enormous butcher and delicatessen. Lynhjems Eftf Ole Jensen in Stengade sells more cheeses than you thought existed. Crepandia is an interesting toy store in the same street and Vin Og Stoger at no. 17 is an antiques shop full of curiosities.

TAKING A BREAK

Axeltorv square in Helsingør is a scruffy square filled with shoppers, cheap cafés and bars and some budget restaurants. For a nicer meal you might try:

Louisiana Café £–££ in the Louisiana museum. Overlooks the sea, with outside tables surrounded by garden statuary. ❷ Louisiana Museum, Gammel Strandvej 13, Humlebæk ❶ 49190719 ❹ 11.00–21.30 Tues–Fri, 11.00–17.30 Sat & Sun

Madam Sprunck ££–£££ An old-fashioned French-style café, bar and restaurant set in a pretty courtyard. A 'tasting' menu allows you to sample five dishes. ❸ Stengade 48, Helsingør ❶ 49264849 ❼ www.madamsprunck.dk ❹ 11.30–00.00 Mon–Thur, 11.30–02.00 Fri, 10.30–02.00 Sat, 10.30–00.00 Sun (kitchen closes 21.30)

If you are out for the day at Bakken there are over 35 cafés and restaurants to choose from and plenty of places for a picnic lunch. In Klampenborg, the town where you alight for Bakken, try:

Peter Lieps Hus £–££ Beautiful thatched roofed house with an interesting history. Outdoor tables for sunny days and good children's menu. ⓐ Dyrehaven 8, Klampenborg ⓣ 39640786 ⓦ www.peterliep.dk ⓛ 10.00–19.30 Tues–Sun

Restaurant Jacobsen £££ Designed by Arne Jacobsen as part of the Bellavista theatre and housing complex. One for a special occasion. ⓐ Strandvejen 449, Klampenborg ⓣ 39634322 ⓦ www.restaurantjacobsen.dk ⓛ 12.00–15.00, 18.00–22.00 Tues–Sat, 10.30–16.00 Sun

ACCOMMODATION

Danhostel Helsingor ££ Hostel set in an old manor house 2 km (1½ miles) northwest of Helsingør. En suite double rooms and dorms. Pleasant nearby beach. ⓐ Ndr Strandvej 24, Helsingør ⓣ 49284949 ⓦ www.helsingorhostel.dk ⓝ Kystbanen: Helsingør, then bus: 340

Hotel Skandia ££ A short walk from the centre of Helsingør. Pleasant, clean rooms with old-world charm. ⓐ Bramstræde 1 ⓣ 49210902 ⓦ www.hotelskandia.dk ⓝ Kystbanen: Helsingør

Hotel Marienlyst £££+ Hotel, casino and spa with views across to Sweden or Kronborg and two top restaurants and bars. ⓐ Ndr Strandvej 2, Helsingør ⓣ 49214000 ⓦ www.marienlyst.dk ⓝ Kystbanen: Helsingør

Roskilde & Hillerød

Roskilde, 30 minutes from the city by train, was once the capital of Denmark and is a quainter, less hectic fjordside city. Its biggest attractions are the Viking Ship Museum and the cathedral, where generations of Danish kings and queens are at rest. Hillerød is a pretty little inland town about 40 minutes from Copenhagen by train, dominated by the fairytale lakeside castle of Frederiksborg. Trains to both towns run at frequent intervals from Copenhagen Central Station, and Hillerød can also be reached by S-train.

For a lively break, come for the four-day Roskilde Music Festival at the end of June or beginning of July.

ROSKILDE

SIGHTS & ATTRACTIONS
Roskilde Domkirke (Cathedral)

A wooden church was first built on this site during the 11th century by a man with the curious, yet oddly modern, name of Harold Bluetooth (Harald Blaatand). In 1170 Bishop Absalon ordered a cathedral to be built, and the east section of the church was completed by the mid-13th century. The rest is an amalgam of later additions made over the following 800 years, and you can clearly see the different parts.

The cathedral is a World Heritage Site and its particular interest, other than its architecture, lies in the side chapels built by various monarchs to hold their mortal remains. On entering the cathedral pick up one of the handouts that list the various side chapels and

Roskilde is dominated by its sober and impressive cathedral

VIKING SHIP MUSEUM

See the workshops, where full-size working versions of
Viking ships are made, the museum island, where hardy
young men and women hack out longboats made from
planks or hollowed out trunks by hand, using original tools,
and the finished boats themselves, fitted out for sea. Around
the workshops are young trees of the species used in the
longboats, and a few stalls have activities for children. There
are sometimes demonstrations of the boats themselves,

⬤ *Nothing matches the thrill of seeing a real Viking ship*

which handle a little as if Laurel and Hardy were sailing them but get under way eventually.

The museum displays five Viking ships found in Roskilde harbour, lovingly reconstructed against a huge glass wall looking out over the harbour. If you or your children fancy it, you can put on Viking clothes and stand inside a mocked-up trading ship or play Viking board games. Good shop.

ⓐ Vindeboder 12 ❶ 46300300 ⓦ www.vikingeskibsmuseet.dk
🕐 10.00–17.00. Admission charge

their occupants. Some of the sarcophagi are plain, austere boxes while others wouldn't be out of place in Tivoli Gardens.

There is also an amusing clock that depicts St George slaying the dragon on the hour, and a 1554 working organ. Upstairs is a museum charting the history of the cathedral, its centrepiece being a replica of a dress worn by Margarethe I (1375–1412). ⓐ Domkirke Pladsen ⓣ 46355814 ⓦ www.roskildedomkirke.dk ⓛ 09.00–17.00 Mon–Sat, 12.30–17.00 Sun, Apr–Sept; 10.00–16.00 Tues–Sat, 12.30–16.00 Sun, Oct–Mar. Admission charge

CULTURE

Museet for Samtidskunst (Museum of Contemporary Art)

Located in the town square of Roskilde and housed in the Palæsamlingerne, a former 18th-century palace, the art here is seriously contemporary. The museum has won widespread acclaim. ⓐ Stændertorvet 3d ⓣ 46316570 ⓦ www.samtidskunst.dk ⓛ 11.00–17.00 Tues–Fri, 12.00–16.00 Sat & Sun. Admission charge

Roskilde Museum

Near to the Palæsamlingerne and accessible using the same entrance ticket is this worthy town museum. It charts the history of Roskilde from prehistoric times right up to the Roskilde music festival. ⓐ Sankt Olsgade 15 & 18 ⓣ 46316500 ⓦ www.roskildemuseum.dk ⓛ 11.00–16.00. Admission charge

RETAIL THERAPY

Shopping in Roskilde, mostly on pedestrianised streets, has a quietly suburban feel to it. The shopping streets are largely for pedestrians only, and there are tables out on the pavements with busy shoppers taking a break. At Rosenhavestrædet 2, Strædet 2 sells some pretty

clothes and soft furnishings. Algade has several interesting shops.
At no. 37 you'll find Butik Jane Onø, selling all sorts of coffee beans,
crockery, candles, cushions, light fittings, perfume, marmalade,
chocolates. Check out Tiger, a store where everything costs 10kr
or 20kr.

The Viking Ship Museum sells Viking-related souvenirs. In an
old gasworks building beside it are two great shops: **Glasgalleriet**
(ⓐ Sankt Ibsvej 12 ⓦ www.glasgalleriet.dk), a craft shop where the
pieces, all glass, are hand-made on the premises, and **Roskildegalleriet**
(ⓐ Hedegade 1 ⓦ www.roskildegalleriet.dk), a warren of galleries
selling the works of local artists.

TAKING A BREAK & AFTER DARK

Next door to Strædet 2 on Rosenhavestrædet is the pleasant Café
Satchmo, good for a cup of coffee and Danish before setting off for
the cathedral. In Skomagergade, the pedestrianised street south
of the cathedral, you'll find any number of good places to stop
for a break.

Rådhuskælderen £–££ In a cellar by the old City Hall, the interior
combines the antique feel, with arched windows and brick walls,
with modern seating and good lighting. Seating outside in summer.
ⓐ Fondens Bro 3 ⓣ 46360100 ⓦ www.raadhuskaelderen.dk
🕑 11.00–23.00 Mon–Sat (kitchen open 11.30–16.00, 17.00–21.30)

Snekken £–££ Close to the Viking Ship Museum and overlooking
Roskilde harbour, with outdoor tables in summer and Danish-
Mediterranean-style food. ⓐ Vindeboder 16 ⓣ 46359816
ⓦ www.snekken.dk 🕑 11.30–23.00 (kitchen open 11.30–16.30,
18.00–21.00)

Gourmethuset Store Børs ££–£££ A fantastic eatery serving home-brewed beer. Choose à la carte or a set menu of anything from two to seven courses. ⓐ Havnevej 43 ⓣ 46325045 ⓦ www.store-bors.dk
ⓛ 12.00–16.00, 17.00–21.30 Tues–Sat

ACCOMMODATION
Roskilde Vandrerhjem £ Ultra-modern hostel with en suite double rooms, family rooms, and views of the harbour. Cooking facilities. ⓐ Vindeboder 7 ⓣ 46352184 ⓦ www.rova.dk

Hotel Prindsen £££ Supposedly Denmark's oldest hotel. Lots of charm. ⓐ Algade 13 ⓣ 46309100 ⓦ www.hotelprindsen.dk

HILLERØD

SIGHTS & ATTRACTIONS
Frederiksborg Slot
Dramatic building set on a series of islands in a man-made lake and surrounded by gardens. Like Rosenborg (see page 108), the site was a summer palace, built in 1560 by Frederik II. Christian IV later added a bigger structure in the Dutch Renaissance style from a design by Hans van Steenwinckel.

In the open courtyard, don't miss the Neptune Fountain, a 19th-century replica of the original that was destroyed during the Swedish occupation. The main body of the castle, destroyed first by the Swedes and then by fire in 1859, is now a museum funded by the Carlsberg Foundation. It charts the history of the Danish Royal Family, with a series of paintings of moments from Denmark's history and portraits of the kings and queens. The chapel, where Danish kings were crowned for nearly two centuries, survived the fire and the Swedes intact and is stunningly ornate, especially when the sun bursts through the stained glass. In the reconstructed Great Hall, look up at the artwork on the ceiling.

The third floor is a national portrait gallery, including a portrait of the present Queen by Andy Warhol. Take a look out of the windows along the northeast wall of the house for beautiful views over the baroque garden. ❶ 48260439 ⓦ www.frederiksborgmuseet.dk ❻ 10.00–17.00 Apr–Oct; 11.00–15.00 Nov–Mar. Admission charge

RETAIL THERAPY

In Hillerød, close by the castle is a craft shop selling patterned jumpers, pottery and the like. The castle shop is well worth a browse too. Slotsgade is a pedestrianised shopping area and the parallel street Herredsvejen contains the shopping centre Slotsarkaderne.

TAKING A BREAK & AFTER DARK

Den Gale Coq £ The atmosphere is best in the evening.
ⓐ Helsingørsgade 16 ❶ 48267545 ❻ 11.00–23.00 Mon–Sat, 11.00–14.00 Sun

Spisestedet Leonora £–££ Located in the castle grounds, this is a convenient stop for lunch à la carte. Danish menu. ❶ 48267516 ⓦ www.leonora.dk ❻ 10.00–17.00 (kitchen open 11.00–16.00)

Slotskroen ££ Traditional Danish dishes in old-world Danish surroundings. ⓐ Slotsgade 67 ❶ 42420088 ⓦ www.hillerodslotskro.dk ❻ 11.30–16.00, 17.30–21.00 Mon–Sat, 10.00–16.00 Sun

Amager

The route from the airport into town by train seems to be a series of building sites as the countryside to the south and east of Copenhagen is developed. The places of interest to tourists in this area are on the flat, culturally distinct island of Amager. This island is linked to Copenhagen by a series of bridges, and now to Malmö in Sweden by Øresundsbroen (Øresund Bridge).

Amager is home to Fields, Denmark's largest shopping centre, as well as the national radio and TV station DR (Danmarks Radio), both located in the newly developed district of Ørestad. As yet, Amager is still a tranquil area, with good beaches along the eastern coastline and some pretty villages, in particular Dragør.

On the western side on reclaimed land is Kalvebod Fælled, a huge nature reserve created during World War II to provide work for Danish men who might otherwise have been transported to Germany to work in the munitions factories. It was used for many years as a firing range before the wildlife park was created. An interpretive centre for the nature reserve offers bikes for hire and use of a campsite in the reserve.

Closer to town is Islands Brygge, a suburb of Copenhagen with an outdoor swimming pool and some nice walks along the waterfront.

SIGHTS & ATTRACTIONS

Amager Strandpark

There has been a beach on Amager's east coast since the 1930s and recreational activities have been going on there for even longer. In the mid-1990s, plans were made to develop the area into a new Strandpark (beach park).

Opened officially in August 2005, this 4.6 km (2.9 miles) futuristic beach boasts an impressive island and lagoon where you will often see kayakers warming up before heading out to sea. In the middle of the island are five 'stations', small innovative designer concrete buildings equipped with spacious and clean toilet and shower facilities, including facilities for the disabled. From the roof there is a fantastic view over the Øresund region.

The northern side of the lagoon is made up of artificial sand dunes while the southern side has a large park for picnics and barbeques. The entire area is protected for recreation purposes only and in summer the place is filled with beach volleyball, kayakers, joggers, basketball matches, puppet shows and more. ☎ 33663336 ⓦ www.amager-strand.dk ⏰ Facilities: 08.00–22.00 mid-May–mid-Sept; 08.00–18.00 mid-Sept–mid-May 🚌 Bus: 12, 5A; metro: Lergravsparken, Øresund or Amager Strand

Dragør

If you want to experience at first hand a complete Danish community in all its *hygge* (cosiness) a good place to visit is the tiny cobbled village of Dragør on the east coast of Amager. Picture-postcard perfect, the village seems fixed in a little time capsule where hollyhocks and tiny pruned bay trees are tended in the cracks between houses and cobbles and the heat of the sun glows off the orange tiled roofs. The village prospered in the 14th century as a fishing port. When steam and diesel powered ships made the sea trade uneconomical for small fishermen, the village emptied and remained untouched for a century or so until improved transport links brought it back into use. The village square is fronted with houses dating back to the late 18th century, while the obelisk at its centre marks the distance from Copenhagen as one and a half

Danish miles. There is a tiny museum close to the harbour containing seafaring memorabilia and a history of the village. The best time to visit Dragør is the last weekend in July or beginning of August for the annual **music festival** (ⓦ www.dragoermusikfest.dk).
Dragør Museum ⓐ Havnepladsen Strandlinien 2 ⓣ 32534106
ⓛ 12.00–16.00 Wed, Thur, Sat & Sun, June–Sept only ⓝ Bus: 30, 32, 73, 350S. Admission charge

Islands Brygge

Walking distance from Rådhuspladsen and Christianshavn, this trendy suburb offers harbour swimming, plenty of comfortable, reasonably priced cafés, take-aways (including bakers, pizza places, and ice-cream) and a few shops and art galleries. It even has its own cultural centre by the harbour. Young Copenhageners head here for the beach-like atmosphere and to hang out at the cafés.
ⓦ www.islands-brygge.com ⓝ Bus: 5A, 250S; metro: Islands Brygge

CULTURE

Amager Museum

Folk museum showing the life and history of Dutch settlers in the 16th century. Set in two old Dutch farms, the museum grows vegetables in the old style, while its curators, dressed in traditional clothes, show you farm processes from cheese and butter making to looking after the animals. The museum is en route to Dragør by road. ⓐ Hovedgade 4 & 12, Store Magleby ⓣ 32530250 ⓦ www.museumamager.dk
ⓛ 12.00–16.00 Tues–Sun, June–Aug only ⓝ Bus: 350S. Admission charge

▶ *The startling Ark Museum of Modern Art*

ARKEN MUSEUM

The Arken Museum for Moderne Kunst (The Ark Museum of Modern Art) is 17 km (11 miles) west of Amager in the working-class suburb of Ishøj, and is a highlight of the area.

Standing on an inaccessible windswept beach reclaimed from Køge Bay, this disorientating museum opened to much acclaim and controversy during Copenhagen's year as European City of Culture in 1996. Designed by architect Søren Robert Lund to look like a giant beached concrete and steel ship, it has a startling effect when viewed from a distance.

The museum has a permanent collection but its chief exhibits are temporary displays, often of very contemporary works, including cinema. Check the website for what's currently on.

The restaurant on the first floor has great views over the bay. The gallery stands on a long reclaimed beach between the towns of Brøndby and Hundige, and is an excellent place for a quiet afternoon.

The museum is easily accessible by public transport.
🚊 Skovvej 100, Ishøj 📞 43540222 🌐 www.arken.dk 🕐 10.00–17.00 Tues & Thur–Sun, 10.00–21.00 Wed 🚆 S-train: Ishøj, then bus: 128. Admission charge

RETAIL THERAPY

Den Blå Hal Copenhagen's largest indoor flea market. Hundreds of stalls of second-hand goods, bric-à-brac and antiques. 🚊 Ved Amagerbanen 📞 20738046 🌐 www.denblaahal.dk 🚌 Bus: 2A, 40. Admission charge

Fields Scandinavia's largest shopping mall, with a huge outdoor terrace where events are held during the summer months. ➌ Arne Jacobsens Allé 12 ➊ 70208505 ⓦ www.fields.dk 🕐 10.00–22.00 Mon–Fri, 10.00–17.00 Sat Ⓜ Kystbanen/metro: Ørestad

TAKING A BREAK & AFTER DARK

There's not much to keep you after dark in Amager. Instead, a short metro ride from the beach and Islands Brygge into the city will take you to the bars and restaurants around Kongen's Nytorv. At Amager beach a few multicoloured beach bars offer drinks and snacks, as do the five concrete stations.

Café Alma £ Good coffee and light meals, including a good vegetarian option and homemade cakes. ➌ Isafjordsgade 5–7, Islands Brygge ➊ 32543204 ⓦ www.cafealma.dk 🕐 11.00–00.00 Mon–Fri, 10.00–01.00 Sat & Sun (kitchen closes 22.00) Ⓜ Bus: 5A; metro: Islands Brygge

⬤ *Islands Brygge is laid-back, even by Copenhagen standards*

Café Saga £ In the heart of the bohemian quarter of Islands Brygge, this café has sunny outdoor seating and reasonably priced meals. Egilsgade 20, Islands Brygge 32571724 www.cafesaga.dk 11.00–23.00 Mon–Fri, 10.00–23.00 Sat, 10.00–22.00 Sun, kitchen closes 21.30, happy-hour 15.00–17.30 Bus: 5A; metro: Islands Brygge

Beghuset ££ Reputedly the best that Dragør has to offer. Comfortable Danish–French cooking and lots of locals. Standgade 14, Dragør 32530136 www.beghuset.dk 12.00–late Tues–Sat (kitchen open 12.00–15.00, 18.00–21.00) Bus 350S

Krunch Restauraunt Kastrup Fortet ££ Organic restaurant with views over Amager beach and the Øresund. Amager Strandvej 246 32845050 www.krunch.dk 12.00–16.00 Bus: 2A; metro: Lergravsparken

ACCOMMODATION

Many of the interesting sights on Amager are a short metro or bus ride from the city, so it is advisable to stay in the centre to make the most of your trip. If you fancy a night or two out of town, the best option is the 100-year-old **Dragør Badehotel** (**££** Drogdensvej 43, Dragør 32530500 www.badehotellet.dk Bus: 350S).

If you're after simple but stylish budget accommodation at Islands Brygge, try **Hotel Copenhagen** (**£** Egilsgade 33, Islands Brygge 32962727 www.hotelcopenhagen.dk Metro: Islands Brygge).

◗ *Not all the police carry light sabres!*

PRACTICAL
information

Directory

GETTING THERE

By air

Ticketless budget airlines are often the cheapest way to travel, especially if you fly off peak. You will find prices are lower the earlier you book; a ticket booked the day before you leave will cost much more than one on the same flight booked weeks in advance. Prices go up during holidays, at weekends and when there is an event on in Copenhagen.

British airports, including London, Birmingham, Manchester, Aberdeen, Glasgow and Edinburgh, have direct flights to Copenhagen, as does Dublin. Flying time from London airports is around 1 hour 45 minutes.

Flights land at Copenhagen Kastrup Airport (see page 48), which has good facilities and fast transport links to the city centre.

Aer Lingus (from Dublin) Ⓦ www.aerlingus.com

British Airways Ⓦ www.ba.com

British Midland Ⓦ www.flybmi.com

Cimber Sterling Ⓦ www.cimber.com

easyJet Ⓦ www.easyjet.com

Norwegian Ⓦ www.norwegian.com

SAS (from UK and Dublin) Ⓦ www.flysas.com

Many people are aware that air travel emits CO_2, which contributes to climate change. You may be interested in the possibility of lessening the environmental impact of your flight through the charity **Climate Care** (Ⓦ www.climatecare.org), which offsets your CO_2 by funding environmental projects around the world.

By rail

This is normally the most expensive way to get to Copenhagen, unless you are visiting the city as part of an Interrail or Eurail trip. **Rail Europe** (Ⓦ www.raileurope.co.uk) can book the journey online.

A direct journey from the UK by rail will first involve a cross-Channel ferry or the **Eurostar** (Ⓣ UK 08705 186186 Ⓦ www.eurostar.com) to Brussels.

The monthly *Thomas Cook European Rail Timetable* has up-to-date schedules for international train services to Copenhagen and many Danish domestic routes. Ⓣ UK 01733 416477; USA 1 800 322 3834 Ⓦ www.thomascookpublishing.com

⬥ *Ultra-modern Copenhagen airport*

By water

If you plan to bring your own car to Copenhagen, you can take the ferry from Harwich, UK, to Esbjerg, Denmark with **DFDS Seaways** (ⓣ UK 0871 522 9955; Denmark 33423000 ⓦ www.dfdsseaways.co.uk). Departures are all year round, three times a week. From Esjberg, the trip by train is about five hours. If you are approaching Copenhagen via Oslo, the ferry takes around 16 hours.

ENTRY FORMALITIES

EU citizens need only a valid passport to enter Denmark, whereas citizens of the US, Canada, Australia and New Zealand need both a valid passport and a return ticket. Visitors from other countries may require a visa and should contact their nearest embassy before travelling. A visa is required by everyone except EU citizens for stays of longer than three months.

Immigration control is strict. Officers may ask for proof that you have a means of support for your stay in the country, that you have somewhere to stay and what the purpose of your visit is.

Residents of the UK, Ireland and other EU countries may bring into Denmark personal possessions and goods for personal use, including a reasonable amount of tobacco and alcohol, provided they have been bought in the EU.

Residents of non-EU countries, and EU residents arriving from a non-EU country, are limited to a maximum of: 200 cigarettes and 50 cigars or 250g of tobacco; 4 litres of wine and 1 litre of spirits.

MONEY

Denmark is not part of the eurozone. Its currency, the krone (kr), is divided into 100 smaller units called øre. Notes come in denominations of 50, 100, 200, 500 and 1,000kr, and coins in 1, 2, 5, 10 and 20kr and 50 øre.

Banks are plentiful. Their opening hours are 10.00–16.00 weekdays, sometimes till 18.00 on Thursdays. There are 24-hour ATMs everywhere and they accept most internationally recognised debit and credit cards. Be careful at weekends as many of them run out of cash. Most banks will exchange a wide range of currencies and you can usually buy items on the plane or ferry in your own currency. Visa and MasterCard are widely accepted in shops and restaurants.

HEALTH, SAFETY & CRIME

No precautions in terms of vaccination or preventive medicines need be taken before visiting Copenhagen. Tap water is safe to drink. Healthcare is good.

EU citizens can use the Danish healthcare system on production of a European Health Insurance Card (EHIC). Note that you may have to reclaim the cost of treatment once you have returned home. A consultation with a doctor as a private patient will cost at least 300kr, usually more.

Emergency treatment is free to all visitors and many countries outside the EU have similar reciprocal agreements. Travel insurance is still essential. Copenhagen is one of the safest cities in Europe, but as always, take care of belongings in crowded places such as the Central Station and Nørreport. Strøget in the early hours may be problematic, and in some areas around Vesterbro and Nørrebro you should be cautious. If you have anything stolen, report it immediately to the police and obtain a copy of their report for your insurance claim. A greater danger to visitors may be the system of cycle lanes, which run along most streets in the city, occasionally against the flow of traffic.

OPENING HOURS

For details of shop opening hours, see page 22. Note that even though most shops are closed on Sundays outside of the summer months, bakeries open on Sunday mornings throughout the year. Office hours, including most banks and post offices, are 09.00–16.00 Monday to Friday. Cafés and restaurants usually close around midnight on weekdays and 01.00–02.00 at the weekends, while clubs usually keep going until around 05.00.

TOILETS

There are a few user-friendly public toilets in Copenhagen. The toilets in Central Station have good and inexpensive showers. Most public squares have pleasant public toilets, as do department stores.

CHILDREN

Copenhagen is an extremely child-friendly city. Most restaurants and café bars have child seats and highchairs and some even have child menus. Trains and buses have areas set aside for buggies and buses have easy access. Bike shops generally hire out children's bikes. The beaches and parks are great for children, especially in summer when there are often puppet shows.

Most museums and art galleries provide special children's sections. Out of town the Akvarium (see page 116) and the Experimentarium (see page 117) have lots of hands-on exhibits, and Louisiana (see page 121) has a children's art room where kids can experiment with different media. Bakken (see page 117) and Tivoli (see page 80) are also likely to keep your kids entertained.

Nationalmuseet (see page 84) has a children's museum and an early school room where they can explore the ink wells. Statens Museum for Kunst (see page 112) has a children's section where children can

⬤ Give the kids a breath of fresh air at the Frilandsmuseet

explore their artistic skills and there are also performances in the lobby.

Orlogsmuseet (see page 100) has a children's section where they can handle guns and climb around a submarine. The Viking Ship Museum in Roskilde (see page 128) has mocked-up ships and dressing up, as well as Viking board games and drawing activities. Tycho Brahe Planetarium (see page 82) is probably more suited to children than adults, particularly the IMAX shows.

You could also try the Guinness World Record Museum (see page 67) or **Ripley's Believe It or Not Museum** (ⓐ Radhuspladsen ❶ 33323131 ⓦ www.topattractions.dk ❸ 10.00–18.00 Sun–Thur, 10.00–20.00 Fri & Sat, Jan–mid-June, Sept–Dec; 10.00–22.00 mid-June–Aug). The open-air **Frilandsmuseet** (ⓐ Kongevejen 100, Lyngby ❶ 33134411 ⓦ www.natmus.dk ❸ 10.00–17.00 Tues–Sun, Apr–mid-Oct ❷ Bus: 184; S-train: Sorgenfri) focuses on Danish rural life, and at weekends children can watch dancing demonstrations, take a ride in a horse and carriage and see costumed farm workers handling the animals.

COMMUNICATIONS

Internet

Internet cafés are a rarity in Copenhagen, since everyone is wired up at home. Most hotels offer free internet connections to their guests. Public libraries have computers with internet access. Try:

Det Kongelige Bibliotek ⓐ Søren Kierkegaards Plads 1 ❶ 33474747 ⓦ www.kb.dk ❸ 10.00–19.00 Mon–Fri, 10.00–14.00 Sat ❷ Bus: 66

Hovedbiblioteket ⓐ Krystalgade 15 ❶ 33736060 ⓦ www.bibliotek.kk.dk ❸ 10.00–19.00 Mon–Fri, 10.00–14.00 Sat

Phone

Public telephones are either coin or card operated. The former take coins from 1kr to 20kr but do not give change. Cards can be bought

TELEPHONING DENMARK

The international dialling code for Denmark is 45. To dial any of the Danish numbers in this book from your own country, dial your own international access code (00 for the UK), then 45, then the eight-digit number. All private phones in Denmark have eight digits and there are no area codes.

TELEPHONING ABROAD

To dial abroad from Denmark, dial 00 followed by your own country's international code (UK 44, Ireland 353, USA and Canada 1, Australia 61, New Zealand 64, South Africa 27) and then the area code (leaving off the first 0) and number.

at S-train stations and post offices. They come in denominations of 30, 50 and 100kr and work out slightly cheaper than using coins. A display in the phone box tells you how much credit you have left. Calls are cheaper after 19.30.

Directory enquiries is 118 and overseas directory enquiries is 113 – be aware that the minute rate is astonishingly expensive for these services. The **Yellow Pages** (Ⓦ www.degulesider.dk) is on the internet.

Post

Letters weighing up to 50g to destinations within Denmark are 5.50kr first class or 5kr second class. The same letter will cost 8kr first class or 7.50kr second class to a European destination, and 9kr first class or 8.50kr second class to the rest of the world.

Main Post Office ⓐ Tietgensgade 37 ⓣ 33754475
Ⓦ www.postdanmark.dk

Central Station Post Office ☎ 80207030 🕒 08.00–21.00 Mon–Fri, 10.00–16.00 Sat & Sun

ELECTRICITY

Denmark runs on 220V 50Hz AC. Danish sockets are round two-pin ones. Adapters are best bought in your home country, since Danish shops sell adapters for Danes going abroad rather than for visitors. Most hotels have square three-pin adapters you can borrow.

TRAVELLERS WITH DISABILITIES

Like most European cities Copenhagen builds new buildings and services with disabled people in mind. Buses have lowering ramps for wheelchairs and the newer hotels will have adapted rooms for disabled guests. Public toilets in newer buildings are disabled-friendly and the metro has lifts and easy access carriages. Older buildings are less accessible.

A free pamphlet is available from the tourist office which lists hotels, restaurants, museums and churches that are accessible to wheelchairs and have other facilities for disabled visitors.

For further information contact **Dansk Handicap Forbund** in Østerbro (ⓐ Kollektivhuset, Hans Knudsens Plads 1a ☎ 39293555 ⓦ www.dhf-net.dk).

TOURIST INFORMATION

Copenhagen Right Now The main tourist information centre in Copenhagen with a café, shop, free internet access and helpful staff who will book accommodation. Lots of free information and maps. ⓐ Vesterbrogade 4A ☎ 70222442 ⓦ www.visitcopenhagen.dk 🕒 09.00–18.00 Mon–Sat, Jan–Sept; 09.00–16.00 Mon–Fri, 09.00–14.00 Sat, Oct–Dec

Helsingør tourist office Useful maps of the town and accommodation information. ⓐ Havnepladsen 3, Helsingør ⓣ 49211333 ⓦ www.visithelsingor.dk

Roskilde & Lejre tourist office Maps, accommodation, free guide to the town. ⓐ Stændertorvet 1, Roskilde ⓣ 46316565 ⓦ www.visitroskilde.com

BACKGROUND READING

The Buildings of Europe: Copenhagen by Christopher Woodward. Illustrated guide to many of Copenhagen's architecturally interesting buildings.

The Complete Fairy Tale by Hans Christian Andersen. Get in the mood for the city with some very weird fairytales.

Copenhagen by Michael Frayn. Strange play which discusses quantum physics, loyalty and betrayal.

Just As Well I'm Leaving by Michael Booth. Some humorous comments on living among the Danes.

Miss Smilla's Feeling for Snow by Peter Høeg. Almost supernatural crime thriller set in Christianshavn.

Seven Gothic Tales by Karen Blixen. The Danish writer's take on the gothic.

A Short History of Denmark by Stig Hornshøj-Møller. Good, brief account of several thousand years of history.

Emergencies

Emergency number for police, ambulance or fire service ❶ 112

MEDICAL SERVICES
Doctor
Your hotel will have a list of local doctors, otherwise go to the hospital. Fees are around 300kr plus and must be paid in cash. Keep receipts if you want to make an insurance claim.

Emergency doctor on call overnight ❶ 70130041 🕐 16.00–08.00

Dentist
The tourist office can recommend a dentist. Dentists' fees are paid in cash.

🔺 *Mounted police ae sometimes seen on the city's streets*

EMERGENCY PHRASES

Help!
Hjælp!
Yehlb!

Can you help me?
Kan du hjæpe mig?
Ka do yehlbeh mai?

Call an ambulance/a doctor/the police!
Ring efter en ambulance/en læge/politiet!
Ring ehfda in ahmboolahnseh/in leh-eh/porlitee-eht!

Emergency dental service (*Tandlægevagt*) 📍 Oslo Plads 14 📞 35380251
🌐 www.tandvagt.dk 🕐 20.00–21.30 Mon–Fri, 10.00–12.00 & 20.00–21.00
Sat & Sun

Hospitals

Skadestuen (Accident and Emergency departments) can be
found at:
Amager Hospital 📍 Italiensvej 1, Amager 📞 32343234
Bispebjerg Hospital 📍 Bispebjerg Bakke 23 📞 35313135
Frederiksberg Hospital 📍 Nordre Fasanvej 57, Frederiksberg
📞 38163522

Pharmacies

Most pharmacies (*Apotek*) keep general shopping hours. You can
recognise them from the sign *Apotek* above the door.
   A 24-hour pharmacy can be found at **Steno Apotek**
(📍 Vesterbogade 6 📞 33148266), opposite Central Station.

POLICE
Near Central Station ⓐ Halmtorvet 20 ⓣ 33251448
Near Kongens Nytorv ⓐ Store Kongensgade 100 ⓣ 33931448

Lost property
The main lost property centre, where all goods are sent after a certain period (usually five days), is **Københavns Politi hittegodskontor** (ⓐ Slotsherrensvej 113, Vanløse ⓣ 38748822 ⓛ 09.00–14.00 Mon–Wed & Fri, 09.00 – 17.30 Thur ⓢ S-train: Islev).

EMBASSIES & CONSULATES
In the event of theft or injury your country's embassy will expect you to go through the emergency channels in Copenhagen. They will also expect you to have taken out travel insurance which will cover your needs. If the emergency is of your own making, such as an arrest for drunk driving or disorderly conduct, the embassy will be unable to intervene. Embassies can, however, issue a replacement passport.

Australian ⓐ Dampfærgevej 26 ⓣ 70263676
ⓦ www.denmark.embassy.gov.au
British ⓐ Kastelsvej 36–40 ⓣ 77348651
ⓦ www.ukindenmark.fco.gov.uk
Canadian ⓐ Kristen Bernikowsgade 1 ⓣ 33483200
ⓦ www.denmark.gc.ca
Irish ⓐ Østbanegade 21 ⓣ 35423233
US ⓐ Dag Hammarskjölds Allé 24 ⓣ 35417100
ⓦ www.denmark.usembassy.gov

ⓞ *Take a canal tour for a different perspective on the city*

Editorial/project management: Lisa Plumridge
Copy editor: Monica Guy
Layout/DTP: Alison Rayner

The publishers would like to thank the following individuals and organisations for supplying their copyright photographs for this book: Adrian Beesley/istockphoto.com, page 71; Nicol Foulkes, pages 7, 9, 17, 24, 30, 65, 69, 74, 79 & 92; Tristan de Haas/istockphoto.com, page 59; Hotel Alexandra, page 36; Hans Laubel/istockphoto.com, page 107; Pat Levy, pages 15, 19, 45, 47, 57, 94, 109, 120, 122 & 141; Eoghan OLionnain, page 152; Tomáš Petrů, page 143; Radisson SAS Royal Hotel, page 39; Cees van Roeden/Wonderful Copenhagen, page 155; Kamil Sobócki/Dreamstime.com, pages 5 & 20; Kenny Viese/istockphoto.com, page 40; Visit Copenhagen, pages 115 & 147; Visit Denmark, pages 13, 21, 62, 81, 111, 127, 128, 137 & 139.

Send your thoughts to
books@thomascook.com

- Found a great bar, club, shop or must-see sight that we don't feature?
- Like to tip us off about any information that needs a little updating?
- Want to tell us what you love about this handy little guidebook and more importantly how we can make it even handier?

Then here's your chance to tell all! Send us ideas, discoveries and recommendations today and then look out for your valuable input in the next edition of this title.

Email the above address (stating the title) or write to: pocket guides Series Editor, Thomas Cook Publishing, PO Box 227, Coningsby Road, Peterborough PE3 8SB, UK.

WHAT'S IN YOUR GUIDEBOOK?

Independent authors Impartial up-to-date information from our travel experts who meticulously source local knowledge.

Experience Thomas Cook's 165 years in the travel industry and guidebook publishing enriches every word with expertise you can trust.

Travel know-how Thomas Cook has thousands of staff working around the globe, all living and breathing travel.

Editors Travel-publishing professionals, pulling everything together to craft a perfect blend of words, pictures, maps and design.

You, the traveller We deliver a practical, no-nonsense approach to information, geared to how you really use it.

Useful phrases

English	Danish	Approx pronunciation
BASICS		
Yes	Ja	*Ya*
No	Nej	*Nai*
Please	Tak	*Tack*
Thank you	Tak	*Tack*
Hello	Hej	*Hai*
Goodbye	Hej hej	*Hai hai*
Excuse me	Undskyld	*Ornskewl*
Sorry	Undskyld	*Ornskewl*
That's okay	Det er i orden	*Di air ee orrdehn*
I don't speak Danish	Jeg taler ikke dansk	*Yai tala ickka dannsk*
Do you speak English?	Taler du engelsk?	*Tala do ehng-ehlsg?*
Good morning	Godmorgen	*Gor-morn*
Good afternoon	Goddag	*Gor-day*
Good evening	Godaften	*Gor-ahfdehn*
Goodnight	Godnat	*Gor-nad*
My name is ...	Mit navn er ...	*Mid nown air ...*
NUMBERS		
One	En	*In*
Two	To	*Tor*
Three	Tre	*Trreh*
Four	Fire	*Feerr*
Five	Fem	*Fem*
Six	Seks	*Sex*
Seven	Syv	*Suw*
Eight	Otte	*Ordeh*
Nine	Ni	*Nee*
Ten	Ti	*Tee*
Twenty	Tyve	*Toova*
Fifty	Halvtreds	*Haltrrehs*
One hundred	Hundrede	*Hoonner*
SIGNS & NOTICES		
Airport	Lufthavn	*Loofft-houn*
Rail station	Togstation	*Toe-stashion*
Platform	Perron	*Perr-on*
Smoking/	Rygning/	*Rooning/*
Non-smoking	Rygning forbudt	*Rooning forboot*
Toilets	Toiletter	*Toiledder*
Ladies/Gentlemen	Dame/Herre	*Dayma/Hair*
Metro/Bus	Metro/Bus	*Meetro/Booss*